'Judith has captured work and life lessons that are relevant not only for women but also for men. In this well-written and easy to follow book, Judith has generously outlined her personal and work experiences. Her book is a must-read for those in the workforce, management, leaders and mentors of any age. Captured in *No Sex at Work* is a rich tapestry of tips which will elevate anyone's career aspirations, performance and outcomes.'

Mark Rantall, CFP, CPA

'A wonderful compilation of lessons and gifts. A career dedicated to delivering incredible opportunities and experiences is encompassed in Judith's words. The examples and insights provided will help all those with the courage, wisdom and mindfulness to use them… There are so many examples but, more importantly, real-life stories that will ensure there should be 'No Sex at Work'. Now it will be up to you to make certain that the journey you're on continues: that you are the change that is needed to make not just your workplace but the world around us a better, more equitable place to be. It starts with you! Because #thebestisyettocome.'

Gary R. Bennett
Executive Chairman & CEO
Northstar Consulting Ltd
(And lots of other things)

'This book is a must-read for anyone, regardless of gender, wanting to take their career into their own hands. Judith has seen it all and is one of the most respected experts in her field. She has a fantastic, no-nonsense approach to sharing practical advice.

'Follow Judith's tips if you want to be a high performer, speed up your career progression and avoid roadblocks (especially the self-imposed ones!). Your career is your responsibility – no-one else's.'

Vanessa Bennett
Next Evolution Performance

'A powerfully modern guide to running a modern career, where Judith rightly identifies creating value as the core competency of leadership.'

Andrea Clarke
Author & Facilitator

'All I can say is WOW – I love it. What a book! I can't wait for the next one. I only wish I'd had this book when I started my career – but it's never too late to learn from Judith's wise words and experience. I plan on adding this to my children's Christmas stockings, as I know my son will benefit as much from this as my daughter. Both are just starting their careers, and I hope they don't make any of the mistakes I made.'

Marisa Broome
Principal, Wealth Advice & Chair,
Financial Planning Association of Australia

'Judith's book fills a critical need in providing insights on how to conduct yourself professionally within the workplace, regardless of gender.

'I congratulate Judith in creating a valuable resource, full of rich content (including some great stories!). It is written for anyone who genuinely wants to progress their career, within a structured framework of proven business and professional protocols. One of the book's key strengths is that it provides valuable advice and perspective about how to navigate through many workplace situations, which at times can seem daunting.

'I have had the good fortune of being guided on many occasions by Judith as I progressed through various roles within the financial services sector. Judith's guidance was always underpinned by her expertise in executive recruitment, and in getting to know the individual she was working with, to ensure the best outcome was achieved at all times.

'Congratulations, Judith, on sharing your invaluable insights.'

George Haramis
Co-Founder at Fiduciary Financial Services Pty Ltd

'If career is important to you, read this book. Judith has been teaching and inspiring people over many years in how to advance their careers and has gifted us yet again by writing *No Sex at Work*. Judith's lessons will help you avoid career pitfalls and assist you to realise your career ambitions, on your terms.'

Ilaine Anderson
Managing Director Workplace Super, AMP

'I have known Judith for more than ten years whilst she ran FRG and FEW and have always taken her advice very seriously. She has been a mentor, an advisor, an advocate and a friend. I know so many people who have benefited from Judith's deep expertise and it's terrific that she has taken the time to condense all her insights into *No Sex at Work*.'

Geoff Rogers
Group Executive Advice (Acting), MLC Wealth

'Absolutely loved it! This is the advice I needed at the start of my career! Judith, you give it your heart and soul. The reflections were a highlight.'

Tizzy Vigilante
Managing Director, Financial Advice, Australia & NZ
IRESS

'Making good choices involves self-reflection, a willingness to challenge our biases and empathy. Judith creates this opportunity as she intertwines her personal stories with insights from her successful career to create a practical and accessible read for both men and women as they start their professional lives.'

Cris Parker
Head of The Ethics Alliance, The Ethics Centre
Director, Banking & Finance Oath

No Sex at Work

Hi Suchandra,

Hope you enjoy NSAW.

Regards Judith

No Sex at Work

IT'S ABOUT LEADERSHIP NOT GENDER:
CAREER TIPS AND STRATEGIES TO THRIVE

JUDITH BECK

First published in 2021 by Major Street Publishing Pty Ltd
E: info@majorstreet.com.au W: majorstreet.com.au M: +61 421 707 983

A catalogue record for this book is available
from the National Library of Australia

NATIONAL
LIBRARY
OF AUSTRALIA

Printed book ISBN: 978-0-6487964-8-0
Ebook ISBN: 978-0-6487964-9-7

Cover design by Tess McCabe
Internal design by Production Works
Printed in Australia by Ovato, an Accredited ISO AS/NZS 14001:2004
Environmental Management System Printer.

10 9 8 7 6 5 4 3 2 1

Contents

Preface

Over the years, many people have asked me why I haven't written a book on my experiences. Having run executive search firm Financial Recruitment Group (FRG) for 25 years and founded membership organisation Financial Executive Women (FEW) in 2012, I have seen it all when it comes to career management. I guess when you are working hard in a field you are passionate about, you're not thinking about taking time out to write a book.

Now that I am towards the end of my career and reflecting on why I was able to achieve what I did without the issues that I see so many people experiencing, I became curious to understand the whys. Why didn't I experience the workplace bullying, sexual harassment or discrimination that I have heard others discussing almost daily? Why was I able to successfully navigate a male-dominated industry? Why did I get business in a very competitive environment when other women were finding it difficult? And why didn't I hit the kinds of glass ceilings other women have?

My inspiration in writing *No Sex at Work* is to help you navigate these kinds of situations, and to share with you some of the do's and don'ts that I have learnt from my own experiences and from mentors and people I respect.

At FRG and FEW I have met and mentored thousands of inspiring, successful executives (men and women) in the financial services industry. I've listened to their concerns and helped them step up and achieve their full potential in their careers – and I've seen where they've gone wrong.

I believe most issues we encounter at work are a result of specific behaviours – it's nothing to do with our sex. The fact that you are a man or a woman shouldn't be relevant in determining your success in the workplace. If you want to be among the top 10 per cent of high achievers in the workplace (what I call the T10Ps), you need to focus on how to get from A to B as a business professional. Don't be side-tracked by the barriers you believe are holding you back due to your sex. The skills needed for business success are the same for everyone.

Keeping sex out of work

You are not a sex at work, you are an individual.

This is the basis for *No Sex at Work*. I know barriers for women still exist in the workplace. On occasion, bad attitudes and assumptions still emerge that seem intent on holding women back. However, I truly believe that we can create our own barriers when they may not even be there. This book is all about helping you to work out how to get around, over or under the real barriers that do exist, not create them when they don't – and arrive at a point where sex is truly not important at work.

My belief is that you are a businessperson first. You must focus on how to get from A to B in your career. The path should be the same for everyone regardless of gender, race, religion, footy club, high school or any other label people try to apply. In this book, I focus on removing the gender label.

Keep sex out of work by:

- building the soft skills you need to handle certain situations in the work environment

- developing the business skills you need to help progress in your career

- highlighting your capabilities as a T10P

- not categorising yourself as a gender, race, religion or any other label society puts on you as an individual or as part of a group.

So, how do you know if sex is currently in play at your work?

If you've found yourself in any of the following situations, you really need to read this book.

- You take a role without negotiating the salary. You say to yourself, 'Don't ask for more money, they will think I am aggressive. I am just happy to get the job'.

- An internal promotion becomes available, but you don't put your hand up. You think your manager would ask you to apply if they thought you were ready. You feel you do not have all the required skills to do the job, and think they'll just hire their buddies anyway, so why waste your time.

- You think business is done on the golf course and you don't play golf, so you feel left out and discriminated against.

- You take a new role where your boss gives you all the clients that no-one wants. You accept it, but you feel it is unfair.

- You are in a meeting with all males and you are asked to take the notes. This makes you angry and you don't know how to respond, so you just do it.

These are just a few examples of sex at work that are experienced every day. How many more have you experienced and how did you handle these situations?

The T10Ps

You will see me refer to the T10Ps throughout this book. These are the top 10 per cent executives – the people who are successful and at the top of their game. They know how to get from A to B in business and they have great soft skills. Sex doesn't even cross their mind at work. They are individuals and they don't allow barriers to be put in front of them – and they certainly don't put any barriers in front of themselves. They all have one thing in common: they follow basic business rules of engagement. When I mention a tip in this book, the action I'm recommending is what the T10Ps do.

You may wonder how I determine who is and isn't a T10P. With more than 25 years in recruiting at senior levels, I have interviewed over 20,000 professionals. I have also consulted to and mentored some of Australia's most successful leaders. This gives me the insight required to see the very clear patterns that highlight why some people are successful and others aren't.

Who do you look up to? What have you observed them doing that makes them successful? These are the people and the actions you should be aiming to replicate.

In the following chapters, I show you how to separate what is direct discrimination and bad business behaviour from your own or others' misconceptions. I include many examples and stories from my life and my 25 years' experience in recruiting, along with points of reflection throughout the book. These points can also be used for your own self-reflection, as you look at how you can apply my experience to your situation. Most importantly, throughout this book I provide you with the tips you need to navigate your career successfully without sex as an issue. This is what I mean by no sex at work.

CHAPTER ONE

No Sex in My House

You've likely heard the old saying, 'Monkey see, monkey do'. As children, we imitate those we see in front of us who become our role models. Our formative years are also commonly believed to have a significant impact on the way we behave as adults.

It isn't surprising that children take after their parents. You don't need to be a psychologist to understand that as adults we influence our children's behaviour for the rest of their lives. I can tell you without a doubt in my mind that my family upbringing influenced most of my behaviours and the way I look at things. Because of my family's influence, I have grown up believing in individuality without focusing on gender biases, especially in the work environment.

REFLECTION

Do you hear yourself repeating something your parents said? Is this something that influenced you to act in a certain way?

I remember very clearly my mother saying, 'There is no time like the present and you only live once'.

I have repeated this to myself so many times in my life. I feel this one sentence helped create the entrepreneurial spirit I have, as well as being the excuse every time I splurge on a new outfit!

My mother also said, 'Wait until you get married, dear'. I didn't listen to this one, which could mean some advice doesn't sink in.

What advice did you take that made a difference in your life? What advice didn't you take that would have been a good idea? What did you learn?

Family sayings live on

Let's look at a few more sayings from my childhood and how they influenced me. Think about whether your parents said any of these to you and if you too were influenced:

- **'The early bird gets the worm'**: My grandmother and father said this one all the time. This was a good statement for me to hear as a child to emphasise that if you want something worth having, you need to get out of bed and go for it.

- **'Work is not easy; that's why they call it work'**: My father would say this one when we complained about doing our chores. I guess the message here is sometimes you need to do jobs you don't like.

- **'Don't put off to tomorrow what you can do today'**: My grandmother would always say these exact words to me when I was indecisive. In later years, I often said this to myself when procrastinating about doing administration work in my business. I would reflect on what Grandmother said and then say to myself, 'Just get it done now and then it is off my list'.

- 'This too shall pass': Another Grandmother saying. I say this when experiencing conflict, because I know everything does pass and things eventually get better.

- 'Things always look better in daylight': My mother would say this when any of my sisters or I were upset about situations happening to us. My take on this was to always take a breath before reacting. In my business, if a problem emerged with a staff member or a client, I would always wait a day to calm down before responding. With a calm mind, you will see things more clearly, and even find another way of looking at a situation.

- 'You need to save for a rainy day': Another one from my grandmother, and I have always lived by this in my businesses. Grandmother would say that things happen when you least expect them, so you need to be prepared and save for a rainy day. I have thanked her in my head so many times when circumstances changed or the economy shifted, and I had money in the bank to ride out the storm.

- 'The squeaky wheel gets the oil': This is probably my favourite one of all time, and my mother, father and grandmother all said it. This has been a staple in my work diet. If you don't speak up, how are people going to know what you want? I often tell women in the FEW membership base that they need to speak up and let their boss know what they want and if anything is bothering them, because people are not mind readers.

These were all positive things that my family said to me. What about the negative sayings we heard as children that influence how we see ourselves and how we act? I asked several of my friends to tell me what they remember their parents saying that influenced them in a negative way, and they provided a few examples. Some of the behaviours I have seen in the past by women I have met could have been the result of this type of childhood influence. These kinds of negative comments include:

- **'Wait until you are asked'**: Hearing comments such as this is possibly one of the reasons women don't put their hands up for jobs – because they are waiting to be asked. I heard this all the time in recruiting when I approached female candidates about why they didn't apply for a role – they would say they were waiting to be asked by their employer. Does this sound familiar? If only they had heard that the squeaky wheel gets the oil!

- **'Don't be so bossy'**: The use (or overuse) of the word 'bossy', especially in relation to women, generated a whole campaign in 2014. This campaign aimed to ban the word, arguing that its use discourages girls and women from seeking positions of leadership. It also makes them self-conscious about speaking up for fear of sounding aggressive. I hope this can be turned around even further and we start telling our girls to be the boss. Be bossy and own it!

- **'Apply for jobs in large companies where you could meet a husband'**: I'm lost for words with this one!!

- **'If it ain't broke, don't fix it'**: I heard this one at almost every job I have gone to. It's a great way to squash creativity or suggestions.

Many more sayings are passed down from generation to generation. What sayings influenced you? Who were your influencers and what impact do they have on you now in the work environment? Did sex play a part?

My family influences

I grew up in a large family. I was the youngest of five girls and one boy. We lived in a middle-class neighbourhood and my father had a good job running a shoe store until I was five. We had a nice house and car, and life was good. Then, when he was in his early forties, my father lost his job, and everything changed.

In those days, men of his age found it hard to find new employment because they were perceived to be 'over the hill'. My father never went to university, because he had been in the air force during World War II. He found not having a degree was another barrier preventing him from getting a job.

He tried selling insurance, but those jobs were commission-based and income was up and down. He just couldn't get anything permanent.

REFLECTION

Think about those times in your life when a crisis, a major change or something unexpected occurred. How did the experience shape you? Was it a wonderful learning experience? Were you thankful that it happened when you reflected on it later? Did those situations have an impact on how you operate at work today?

For example, my father losing his job could have influenced my need to be financially independent.

During this time, I saw my father being persistent and getting in front of potential employers. He didn't lie around the house and hope something would come to him. He would look in the paper every day and cut out the employment ads and get on the phone. Time after time, he was knocked back and he knew it was his age or not having a degree or both, but he still kept trying.

Children witness similar examples of this all the time, often without their parents realising the influence it has. Are they teaching resilience or how to give up?

We have all heard the saying, 'Actions speak louder than words'. Did you learn resilience from your parents, or do you have a habit of giving up early?

Eventually we lost the house my parents were paying a mortgage on, and they almost went bankrupt. My grandmother encouraged them to move back to her neighbourhood and rent a house up the street so she could help with babysitting.

Months went by with no income. I remember the landlady knocking on the door for rent and my parents pretending no-one was home. My parents argued about money and it was sad seeing my dad losing confidence. We saw his funny teasing sense of humour less and less.

In happier times, my father would always make a tense situation lighter by making a joke of it. If I were upset or having a tantrum, as kids do, he would say something like, 'It's not the end of the world and if you think this is bad, you ain't seen nothing yet'. That was his way of telling me to get over it.

REFLECTION

How do you react in hard times? How much of how you react do you believe comes from your parents? Are you paying attention to how your own behaviours are being perceived?

I believe seeing my parents struggle financially motivated me to make sure it didn't happen to me. In my mind, lack of money to pay bills would cause arguments and could put a strain on a good relationship.

One thing my parents never did was feel sorry for themselves or blame others for their hardship; they just kept trying. Seeing this has made me a fighter in times when things have not gone my way. I also don't blame others for my mistakes.

If you make mistakes or things aren't going your way, do you blame others? What can you do to take responsibility?

Before this, my siblings and I had all been going to a private school; however, with no money coming in we had to change to the public system. My grandmother made sure I went to a Catholic school until eighth grade but, after that, my parents would no longer accept her continuing to pay for my school fees. They insisted I go to the public high school my siblings already attended.

While I was devastated when I had to move schools because I wouldn't know anyone, I soon settled into the new school and loved it. With hindsight, attending public school prepared me to be able to interact with people from all walks of life, and I learnt to look at things from diverse perspectives. I really was very fortunate to have that experience.

REFLECTION

Were you exposed to others from diverse backgrounds when you were growing up? Do you feel comfortable with different perspectives now, or thrown by them?

Going to the public school after being in a private school was a huge change in my world. The high school I went to had every nationality and socio-economic group represented. About 40 per cent of the students at the school were from African and Hispanic backgrounds. In contrast, the Catholic school had at most two or three non-white students. I was so fortunate to be able to make friends from diverse backgrounds, and these friends gave me a different perspective on things and opened my mind to other possibilities. I believe this also helped me with my no sex at work attitude.

How has your experience of different backgrounds and perspectives shaped how you relate to others in the workplace?

My mother, the boss

Until my father lost his job, my mother had managed the house. Even in those days, it cost a lot to raise six children, and that was without indulging them with the latest brands and gadgets. As the youngest of six, I rarely got anything new; most of my clothes and toys were handed down.

Now with no income, my mother needed to think of creative ways to make what little money we had last. She managed to make meatloaf with oatmeal and veggies feed everyone for several days. There were days when we only had popcorn to eat for dinner because it was so cheap.

In times of adversity, you learn to make use of what you have, and my mother was great at making things stretch. Maybe her upbringing during the Great Depression and World War II taught her how to be grateful for what she had and to make the best of everything.

After over a year of my dad not being able to find a job, however, I think my mother just said to herself, 'Enough is enough. If he can't find a job, I will'.

Even though my mother was also in her forties, she was attractive and looked as if she were 30, and this proved an advantage. She easily found a job demonstrating products in retail stores, home shows and fairs. She also had a natural talent for speaking to people and proved she was a great salesperson. My mother quickly became the main breadwinner in our family.

Her boss found out very quickly how good she was but still thought he could pay her less than the men. When she found out from her male co-workers that she was being paid less, even though she was the top-performing salesperson, she confronted her boss. His response was, 'Yes, but they have families to support'. My mother shot back, 'What do you think I have!' Shortly after that, she quit.

Back then, women were treated as second-class citizens. Few people, and especially not women, would speak back to a boss. For my mother to do that showed a real sense of self-worth and confidence.

Looking back, I am sure we would have all said, 'Yeah, Mum!' It wouldn't have been unusual for us kids to see her stand up for herself because that was her nature. Even though my mother was always polite, she wouldn't think twice about speaking her mind.

You can still be polite and get your point across.

After working for another employer for a few years, my mother developed the confidence to go out on her own and build her own network of demonstrators working in retail stores and home shows. No discussions in the household led me to believe this was unusual. I heard no comments that women shouldn't run a business; it just happened, and everyone accepted it – including my father.

My mother got my dad involved with the new business, so he was now working for her.

REFLECTION

What was your first job and what did you learn from it?

My mother also had all of us kids working in the business during school breaks. This provided me with the foundation experience I needed in dealing with people as customers. We often would work from seven in the morning to ten at night, which also introduced me to a hard day's work.

We were always paid for the work we did and never expected to work for free. This provided us kids with a cash flow. Our parents never told us how to spend our money. My mother would simply say, 'Spend it wisely because when it's gone, it is gone and there is no more where that came from until it's earned'.

How did your earliest work experiences shape your work ethic and attitude today?

Seeing my mother calling the shots showed me that a woman could be the boss. Her actions also showed me that you could be a boss without being aggressive or shouting at people. She didn't let people take advantage of her good nature, however, and was always firm but fair.

I also learnt what it was like when business was good and when it wasn't. Some of the products my parents sold were not winners. With each product failure, my mother had to re-focus and search for a new product they could sell. Eventually they found the right one. For the next 25 years, they sold non-stick cookware until they retired at 80. I think this showed me you may have to try a few things before you get it right but you should never give up.

Even though my mother's business had ups and downs, our situation was never again as bad as when my dad didn't have a job.

My father had to adapt

My father was never intimidated by my mother working and bringing in money when he couldn't find a job. They were a team. While she was working, his job was taking care of us. Very 2020s if you think about it!

While his self-confidence was affected by not being able to provide financially for his family, he was resilient enough to adapt and make the best out of what was in front of him. He didn't take his failure to get a job out on my mother; he accepted that work for him would now be different. He was no longer the boss, but that was okay.

My father would always discuss things openly at the dinner table with my mother. Having this open communication meant I was listening and learning at the time without knowing it. Children pick up on what the adults are saying, so if you have conversations demonstrating equality, chances are this will set a good example for the ones listening. My parents rarely spoke behind closed doors, and we heard everything – sometimes maybe too much!

Even though my father would joke that children should be seen and not heard, we were a loud family. Everyone had an opinion and speaking up was not an issue. When you are the youngest of six, you also learn to speak up or you will be drowned out. That didn't mean that we could interrupt our parents. Manners were high on the list, and my father would be quick to let you know if you were out of line.

Money was extremely tight when my dad wasn't working. He couldn't afford a nice car so he drove an old red and white one with a green fender. He couldn't afford to paint it and it barely worked. I was embarrassed to be seen in it, so I would ask him to drop me off a block before school. Looking back, I realise that must have made my dad feel terrible.

REFLECTION

How comfortable was your family when you were growing up? Could your family afford everything they needed, or was life more of a struggle?

At 19, I took out my first loan for a new car. All my life I have been car-obsessed. Would I be so obsessed if my dad had driven a nice car? That green fender made such an impact that the memory is so vivid, even today. The only difference now is that I feel ashamed about having him drop me off a block before school. I am proud of my dad for the way he handled a tough situation. I should have just been grateful for the ride to school and not worried about what people thought. How many times have you been worried about what others think and as a result hurt the feelings of someone you care about?

I believe my father was supportive when it came to equality in the family because his mother was strong. His mother is the grandmother I refer to in this book. He grew up seeing a woman being in control and working equally with her husband. In fact, I believe my grandmother was the boss in their family. My father never spoke back to her and if she wanted something done, he did it with no questions or complaints. He had an older sister who ran her own restaurant who was also strong. His upbringing no doubt influenced what we were taught.

How did your childhood influence your ideas on financial security? Did you see good or more negative examples of equality between men and women?

My grandmother

I was very lucky to have a strong grandmother who lived just up the street, and she became a big influence on me as well. When my grandfather died, I asked my mother if I could live with Grandma for a year to keep her company. My mother was working, so I would always go to Grandma's house after school anyway; it wasn't a big adjustment.

My grandmother was entrepreneurial for her time and rented out her large house as apartments and single rooms to the military men returning from overseas. She charged extra for making them dinner and doing their laundry and cleaning. Nothing was provided for free and they understood right from the beginning that she was a good businessperson; they knew not to mess with her.

She was a 5 foot 2, 100 per cent proud Irish Catholic woman who ran her own race; a strong woman who never let anyone tell her what to do. She was nice, funny and always got her way.

Grandma's favourite saying was, 'You catch more bees with honey'.

She always went the nice route first and gave people a second chance, but if she didn't get what she wanted – watch out! There'd be no more honey and the bee would sting!

I watched how she dealt with people and felt she was always fair and would listen to others' views, but she was also firm on her convictions. People never crossed her, because she had a way of putting you in your place with a very stern tone that would make you feel two feet tall.

Grandma was so confident that when she walked into the room, you knew it. She wasn't especially attractive, but knew how to dress and look the best she could. When she was older, she was as wide as she was tall but that didn't matter; she commanded attention and respect, and she got it. Her attitude and confidence got her everything she wanted.

I remember when we went to church, my grandmother would always make a beeline for the front row. Often, we would be the only ones in the front while every row behind us was full. She loved it, and I think it made her feel in control and important.

During the service, my grandmother would sing louder than anyone else, even though she couldn't hold a tune. She would also pray louder – and if that wasn't bad enough, she was always a step ahead in the song or prayer than everyone else. Maybe she thought God was a man and so she better let him know she meant business and not to underestimate her! I was embarrassed at the time, but now realise it was just Grandma living life on her own terms. Also, she should have known that God is a woman and there was no need to shout! ☺

REFLECTION

Why is it that no-one wants to sit in the front row? Anyone who has spoken at events will notice that few people go willingly to the front row – and especially women.

One time when I was the keynote speaker, I instructed the ushers to take the front row of chairs away after the second row was filled. I could see people were uncomfortable with their new front-row position. At the beginning of the presentation, I then told the story of my grandmother always going to the front row.

I wanted to make people think about their discomfort. Why do we feel we can't go to the front? Does it come from our school days of not wanting to be asked a question and be put on the spot? Or do we want to duck out early without being seen if the speaker isn't good?

Remembering my grandmother now, I wonder: how many times do we shy away from making our voice heard? How many times do we worry about what other people think, and feel judged for just being ourselves?

My advice to you is to speak up! Sit in the front row and be seen. If you are asked a question you don't know, just say you don't know. It's not the end of the world. If you must leave early, then yes, sit in the back.

Lessons learnt in the home

I think it is very important for parents to think about the messages we give our children. What are they taking with them when they leave home? How are we going to make them resilient? I learnt some very clear lessons from my childhood.

Make your own money and then you will have choices

One time, a friend of my grandmother said to me, 'It is just as easy to marry a rich man as a poor man'. That made my grandmother so mad that she took me aside and said, 'Make your own money, then you will have choices'.

I liked that idea, and the suggestion that a man could be a financial plan also annoyed me. I was determined to never, ever ask someone for money. I wanted my own money, and I wanted those choices my grandmother spoke about. To this day, I can't think of anything worse than not being able to control what I spend.

My grandmother especially instilled in me that no-one is better than you. She said people have different jobs and skills and that you need to find what you are good at. If someone is a movie star, they are good at remembering lines and showing emotion in the delivery of their lines. That is their skill and they shouldn't be put on a pedestal – it just means they are good at their job.

I think this is one of the reasons I have never levelised people (more on levelising later). I've never been starstruck. If I met the Queen of England, I would shake her hand and be as respectful with her as I would with anyone else, but I would not be prepared to curtsey. I really like her and respect her, but she is just a person; she isn't better or worse than anyone else.

REFLECTION

Did you start earning your own income as quickly as you could? How did your first experience of employment shape you?

Along with working for my parents during the school holidays, I also worked part-time after school in retail. I already knew that if I wanted to have my own income, I needed a job. Working gave me freedom to be able to fund my entertainment.

When you are young, you do the jobs you are given – usually the ones the more experienced staff don't want to do. My grandmother and parents would say that to get anywhere you need to start at the bottom or the beginning. Be grateful for the opportunity and learn everything you can about the business. If you do a good job, you will be noticed and rewarded. I believe this stands true today.

Their guidance equipped me to handle many situations during this time as a young employee. The lessons I learnt from my grandmother and parents meant I wouldn't put up with bad behaviour to keep a job.

Did you experience bad behaviour in your early jobs? How did you deal with it? Did you call it out or were you too afraid to say anything?

Equality is learnt

I was lucky enough to learn about equality and resilience and have the confidence to stand up for myself from seeing my mother standing up to her boss for paying her less than her male colleagues.

I have never once been scared to leave a job or speak up if I felt something wasn't right. Maybe if my mother had displayed different behaviours and had accepted being paid less than her male colleagues as 'just the way things are', I would have felt fearful if I had faced a similar situation myself.

During my childhood, I never once felt that I was any less capable than my brother or boys in general. I was taught that I could do anything I put my mind to. Although we were poor, this wasn't a roadblock to success.

Some gender stereotypes applied when chores were divided, with my brother having to do outside yard work and us girls having to do the inside chores. However, if we had been over six foot tall like my brother maybe it would have been different!

All of us siblings were taught that nothing is for free and money doesn't grow on trees. We had to earn our way.

We were never taught that girls were any different from boys when it came to choosing a career. This meant that, when I started my first job, I didn't think of myself as a particular gender. I had no idea about sex at work.

I focused on the skills I needed to develop to progress within my career. Gender stereotypes didn't cross my mind at the time, so I didn't feel suppressed because of my sex.

All my sisters went to university and became professionals. I have never heard them complain about sex at work, discrimination or any gender-related issues. Again, I'm not saying these issues don't exist. However, I do believe the attitude and approach you choose go a long way to combating them. I wouldn't mess with my sisters: anyone who does will quickly find out they can stand up for themselves, and that's because of what they learnt growing up.

My oldest sister became a judge, and she would have been appointed at a time when there were very few women judges. Why did she succeed? Why did I succeed, and my other sisters?

Maybe it's because we were taught to respect and stand up for ourselves.

Our mind is the only roadblock

When it comes to sex at work, I believe our minds are the only things getting in the way of us achieving what we set out to achieve.

It is amazing that adversity can sometimes spark things within us that we didn't know we had. For instance, if my dad had kept his job, my mother would have continued to be a housewife in the traditional way that was common in those days. How would that have changed my perceptions of what women can and can't do? I wonder if I would have turned out differently.

> **Whatever role you take in your family and career, it is important to be in control of your destiny and not be limited in what your dreams are.**

Your sex should in no way control what these dreams are.

Let's now look at how we can take what we have learnt growing up and either fine-tune or undo behaviours to ensure our success at work as an individual and to become a T10P.

CHAPTER TWO

No Sex in Your Job Application

Whether you're applying for a position for the first time in your career or the first time in years, it can be tricky to know how to start.

You might become stressed at the very thought of putting yourself out there in your job application, as your imposter syndrome/self-doubt kicks in (see chapter 6 for more on this). You might feel that the company always hires men, or that if they choose a woman they are only doing so to fill a quota, so why bother.

Let's take sex out of the process and look at applying for the role because it excites you, and because your capabilities as an individual are a good match for it. Don't go into the application and interview process with a preconceived idea about the gender you think the company wants. Start looking through another lens. In my role as an executive recruiter, not once did I feel that my clients were discriminatory about who they wanted for the role. The focus was to get the best person for the job: they wanted T10Ps and gender didn't matter.

In this chapter and the next, I run through everything I observed as an executive recruiter that the T10Ps did to create an outstanding job application, secure an interview and conduct a good interview. In other words, I tell you why they were successful in getting the job.

Who cares how many boxes you tick?

Women often tell me that they feel they should meet at least 70 to 80 per cent of the key selection criteria for a role before they will apply. In contrast, guys will apply even if they only tick two to four of the requirements. In fact, men often don't care how many boxes they tick. If they are interested in the role, they go for it.

The guys are right, ladies! Just go for it. What have you got to lose? You won't get the role if you don't go for it. Don't look at how many boxes you tick; look at your capabilities and capacity to grow in the role. If you're considering a more senior role, remember this: because of the shortage of women in senior roles, women are unlikely to have direct experience in the role. So you need to look at capabilities.

REFLECTION

How many times have you told a recruiter you were not interested in an opportunity, before you heard them out?

When I was headhunting, I noticed a definite difference in the reaction I received when I approached men and women.

The female candidates would consistently say (before I even had the chance to tell them what the opportunity was), 'Thanks Judith, but I am happy where I am and I'm not interested'. I would reply, 'I know you are happy – I am not calling the miserable people. But until I tell you about the opportunity, how do you know you are not interested?' I would then need to persuade them to meet me for a coffee to hear more about the role.

With the male candidates, I would say who I was, and they would reply by asking me to wait while they closed their office door. They would also say that they were happy; however, that would be followed by, 'It doesn't hurt to have a coffee and find out more'.

The male candidates were open to listening to every opportunity. If, after hearing about the role, they didn't want it, they would refer someone they thought would be good. The women rarely referred others.

I noticed this happening for internal positions as well. Women would tell me that they didn't want to leave their current role because they were in the middle of something, and the timing was not right. FYI – the timing is never perfect!

The reason for these differences had nothing do with inherent gender characteristics and everything to do with having mentors in your corner, which I discuss in chapter 8.

Think about how you have approached opportunities in the past. Could you have handled the situation differently and maybe opened the door to a new opportunity? If you knocked back a position, did you refer someone you know for it? If not, why not?

When I was conducting internal interviews for clients, they would often ask me to interview male candidates who did not meet the requirements for the position. The client would say something like, 'Put John through the process. He isn't experienced enough for the role, but he applied, so let's see how he goes'.

John would go through the process ticking only two boxes; however, he would make a good impression and build his profile with several managers in the company who he had not met before the interview. The hiring manager would come back and say, 'John did a great job. He still doesn't have enough experience for this role, but let's keep him in mind for other roles in the future'. John is now on the radar.

I also noticed that even when the guys didn't get the role they first applied for, they would persevere and continue to interview for the next opportunities within their organisations.

Someone like John would continue to apply for internal roles before eventually landing a promotion, for which he ticked six out of ten boxes. A woman in his position would still be waiting to tick eight boxes before applying, and would more than likely be reporting to someone with less experience and teaching him what she knows.

I also found that when the female candidates were unsuccessful in getting a role, their confidence would plummet and it would be a long time before they put themselves out there again. They said it was too disappointing, and they often felt the process was unfair because they didn't see the person who got the role as better than them. If they did go for another role, someone in the organisation would often need to tap them on the shoulder specifically for that next opportunity.

If you see an internal role you are interested in, you should apply. The company will tell you if you are not suited, but at least you have signalled to your employer that you are interested in advancement.

REFLECTION

Don't ignore internal opportunities or have preconceived ideas about them!

When I was running FEW, I heard about a management role with one of our clients. One of our members was in that team and would be perfect for the role. I called her up and asked her if she was going to put her hat in the ring. Her immediate response was, 'No, they always go external, so why bother?' I told her she would be very annoyed if she ended up reporting to (and training) one of her colleagues with a lot less experience than her.

I said, 'No argument – you are going for this role and we will help you.' I got her to speak to her FEW advocate, who encouraged her, and I helped her with the interview process. During the interview, a member of upper management said to her he was surprised to find out she was interested in management roles, and was pleased to see she was.

In this case, her company didn't go external and she was one of two candidates on the final short-list. The position was put on hold due to the economic environment; however, she ended up getting the promotion she wanted a few months later because of that process.

Misperceptions that the company will go external to find candidates is often a barrier people put up – and this self-imposed barrier means they miss out on opportunities. Female and male T10Ps never put up barriers. They don't second-guess; they just go for it.

Remember – companies only ever go to the expense of external recruitment if they have no internal applicants. If you don't put your hand up, you will never know where you stand.

No sex in your resume – just results

So, you have decided to go for a role and now you need to get your resume to the hiring manager. Whether this is your first full-time role, or a more senior role you've had your eye on, the importance of a good resume never changes. I have seen many styles for resumes and the golden rule I would always recommend is keep it simple.

I don't go into great detail on creating a resume here, because you can get dozens of templates off the internet to help you. However, as a past headhunter, I run through what I liked to see on a resume.

Front page

Here's what you should include on the first page of your resume:

- **Personal details:** Include your name, contact number, email, and your LinkedIn profile link. Use a private email address if you are going for external roles.

- **Career summary:** Keep this to one to two paragraphs at the most. The summary is similar to your elevator pitch, so keep it simple and to the point, providing a quick snapshot of your experience and capabilities.

- **Education:** Often people leave this until the last page of their resume; however, if you have degrees, put the details, including date completed, on the front page. If you haven't completed the qualification in full, make sure you state the level you reached. Don't try to make it look like you have a degree when you don't.

- **Summary of employment:** List your current employer first, including start date. Do not fudge any dates because they will be checked at reference stage, so ensure they are absolutely accurate for every role. Do not add extra months to a job period because you want to fill a gap in your resume when you were unemployed. If you have a gap in unemployment, put those dates in as well and state the reason – for example, paternity leave, long service leave, travel or study.

Page two - history of employment

Include your more detailed history of employment on the next page of your resume, keeping in mind the following:

- **List your current role first, followed by previous roles:** Provide a short summary of your current role and then list responsibilities in bullet form, followed by achievements in bullet form. Then list previous roles, including similar information. The last two to three roles will be the most important if they're within ten years, so put more detail in. After ten years, you can be brief.

- **Include short-term roles:** Do not leave out a short-term role because you think it will look bad. Everyone has a short-term role in their career at one stage or another. Be honest about it and don't try to cover it up. It is a big but small world and will come out eventually. I cover how to address short-term roles in the interview in the next chapter.

- **List additional information:** If you have additional information such as your interests, these should be added last. Only include them if they are relevant for the role or say something interesting about you that you want the interviewer to know – for example, accomplishments outside of work.

The following is an example of a great career summary from the resume of Anna Siassios, who was my fabulous Head of Marketing and Operations Manager at FEW.

CAREER SUMMARY

With 12 years' experience in financial services, fin tech and educational industries, I have developed advanced relationship skills with the ability to gain trust through identifying needs, communicating clearly, negotiating on expectations and delivering on what's promised. I have a strong passion for client/ member experience, leading to retention.

I have a diverse set of transferable skills in project management, stakeholder relationships, member experience, brand marketing and communications, leadership, conferences and events, strategic planning and execution, HR and operations.

With an optimistic outlook and collaborative leadership style, I share knowledge and encourage team success, enabling my people to excel under pressure and meet tight deadlines. I work best in a team-oriented culture where everyone is working towards the same outcome.

I have also taken a sample section from Anna's employment history in her role at FEW as an example of how you can list responsibilities and achievements.

FINANCIAL EXECUTIVE WOMEN (FEW)
October 2016 – July 2020

FEW is a member-based organisation that provides women within professional and financial services a community that will train, guide, and support them for the duration of their career journey. Our flagship advocate program is embedded into some of Australia's most successful companies.

Head of Marketing and Operations

Managing a small team of two direct reports, I was responsible for retention of 17 corporate partners and 900 members nationwide. My role encompassed the following business functions: events, marketing, communications, member experience, managing relationships with program managers, human resources, business planning and operations.

Responsibilities:

- Brand member experience for 900 members nationally, from onboarding to advocate pairing
- Retention of corporate partners
- Marketing function – brand, social media, communications, PR
- Responsible for marketing budgets, P&L and ROI
- B2C marketing campaigns
- Management of the FEW leadership conferences

Listing your achievements - and following the 'so what?' principle

When you list an achievement on your resume, make sure you follow the 'so what?' principle. If someone still needs to ask 'So what?' after the statement, you haven't said enough.

For example, if you put on your resume:

I developed a new technology platform for the company.

So what? It could have been the worst platform in the world that introduced errors and caused problems. In other words, you haven't included the complete story.

Saying the following instead is much stronger:

I developed a new technology platform for the company that improved productivity by 50 per cent and saved the company $100k.

That is a statement of an achievement with a result. The reader will immediately feel they have someone who produces a quantifiable result.

If you take one thing away from this chapter, it is to look at your resume right now and do the 'so what?' test with your achievements and put in the results for each statement.

Let's take another look at Anna's resume to see how this works in practice:

ACHIEVEMENTS

- Successfully led team through 2019 annual leadership conference with 300 in attendance, produced on budget 86NPS, 15% uptake of new members through membership drive.

- Successfully led 2018 annual leadership conferences, with five national conferences run over a two-month period, managing 48 speakers, five separate agendas, five working groups leading to the success of conference and overall score of 9.04/10. This initiative also contributed to our business onboarding 300 new members, and increased brand awareness in Brisbane, Adelaide and Perth.

- Our Circle session member initiatives had 400 women attend nationally, increasing attendance by 60% from 2017.

- Increase in social media following on LinkedIn by 65%.

- Improved administration process for membership sign-up, increasing productivity by 50%.

In my experience, men usually pass the 'so what?' test and quantify their achievements. Often women don't list anything as an achievement on their resume. Because I knew this was common with resumes from women, I needed to look past this and interview them to find out the real story. This should not be something that divides the sexes.

Don't forget your cover letter

No matter the job you're applying for, every resume needs to be sent with a cover letter that is tailored to the application. Don't do all the hard work getting your resume right just to have your cover letter let you down. This may sound harsh but attention to detail is very important and makes an impression. You will be rejected by hiring managers if you don't take the time to get the cover letter correct. They will likely wonder what else you will present with errors on it.

Have your cover letter checked by a fresh eye and make sure you keep the following in mind:

- Don't address the hiring manager as 'Sir' or 'Madam' – find out the name of the person you are sending the application to. If this is not possible, say 'Dear Hiring Manager'. Do not be casual and just use something like 'Hi' or 'Hey'.

- Make sure you have the right position and all details are correct.

- Tailor the cover letter for the position you are applying to. It should all fit on one page. Include a short explanation on why you feel you would be the right person for the role.

Four aspects stood out for me when deciding to short-list candidates who sent me their resume and cover letter:

1. **Professional presentation:** Spelling mistakes and grammatical errors were a red flag, so make sure you have a fresh eye look at your resume and cover letter before sending.

2. **Clarity about positions held:** Keep your resume simple and to the point. No drawn-out paragraphs padded with buzz words for every role.

3. **Achievement-oriented:** I wanted to see what candidates had accomplished and if they were goal-oriented. For example, someone in sales not stating their achievements would be a red flag. Every role should have achievements, either geared toward quantifiable numbers and percentages, or towards productivity and process improvements.

4. **A good summary:** I also wanted to get a picture of who candidates were, so a good summary describing their background and what they are passionate about was important.

Preparing for the interview

You get a call saying you are on the long-list for a role and they would like to organise an interview. No matter what level you are interviewing for, follow all their directions and be courteous to everyone in the process.

> **Remember – every person you speak to in the process is a stakeholder and will give their opinion to the hiring manager.**

Don't 'levelise' and always remember the common courtesies. (See chapter 4 for more on what I mean by 'levelise'.)

REFLECTION

Do you treat people differently depending on their role? Or do you use the same courtesy with everyone?

Over the years, I have seen many people miss out on jobs or internal promotions based on feedback a personal assistant or administration staff member gave to the hiring manager.

In one instance, I was part of an interview panel for a general manager position. The final interview was with the managing director and the panel. It was the MD's assistant's responsibility to book all the interviews.

After interviewing two of the candidates, the MD said to his assistant, 'I don't seem to have a time booked in my diary for candidate X'. She replied, 'I have been trying to get him booked in, but it took forever for him to return my call and when he did, he couldn't make any of the available times and said he would get back to me'.

The MD said that for a job of this nature, the candidate should have made the effort. He asked me to take him off the final short-list.

Often candidates in this kind of situation never know why they didn't get the role. They are given the standard line: 'It was very close, all candidates were great, and we will keep you in mind for the next one'.

This is a prime example of why you need to make a good impression with everyone you interact with, no matter your sex or theirs.

The interview process will often have several layers; the more senior the role, the more layers. Some roles at senior levels could take three to six months to finalise, with up to ten interviews and with several stakeholders. This is a long time to dedicate to a process, but good things are often worth putting the time into.

When preparing for your interview, here are five tips I recommend for every interview:

1. **Research the company and the interviewer/s:** You should know everything about the company, the division and the interviewer/s that you are interviewing with. Even if you are currently working at the company, don't make the mistake

of not refreshing the details on products and services – including what is working and what isn't.

If you're not currently working at the company, look up all the managers on LinkedIn and Google. Look at the company website as well as the websites of major competitors – what are competitors doing and what sets the company you are interviewing with apart? You cannot over-prepare.

If you know who was in the position previously, look them up on LinkedIn. Look at their background and how long they were in the role. If they were in the role only a short time, add this to the list of questions you want to ask the interviewer – why did the last person leave the role so soon? See if you can find out who the last two people were in that role and see if you notice a pattern or any red flags.

2. **Review your resume the night before:** Make sure you have all the facts of your history and your achievements clear in your mind. This will mean you can avoid saying in the interview, 'It's on my resume'. This is annoying and you probably will not get a second interview. Interviewers know it is on your resume – they want to hear it from you.

3. **Always plan to be early and give yourself more time than needed:** Being rushed will cause extra pressure. You may come across as being nervous if you have had to rush to get to an interview or are worried that your meter will run out because the interview is going over time. It is never acceptable to be late to an interview so make sure you are there at least 15 minutes early. This will also give you time to settle and to make a good impression with the receptionist by practising common courtesies.

4. **Treat every interview as the first interview:** Make the same effort for every interview as you did for the first one.

You wouldn't want to go from being the preferred candidate to the least preferred because of something you said or did.

5. **Prepare questions to ask during the interview:** Remember an interview is a 'two-way street'. The employer will try to determine through questioning if you have the qualifications and skills necessary to do the job. You must also determine through questioning whether the role will provide the growth and development you seek.

Preparing for online interviews

One of the (many) impacts of the COVID-19 pandemic is the increased use of online interviewing for candidates. I predict this will become the norm, even after things are back to some kind of normal. Online interviews are a great way for recruiters and hiring managers to conduct first interviews and save time.

Along with the tips we have already discussed, online interviews have additional preparation requirements you should be aware of. Don't underestimate the online interview process, and preparation is just as important. Keep in mind the following:

- **Ensure your office is set up well:** Get rid of clutter in the background. If your office is in a bedroom, find a wall to sit in front of where you don't see the bed. Ensure the computer is at eye level, so you are looking into the computer as if the person is directly in front of you. Ensure you are not sitting too close to the camera – otherwise, you could look like an egg with eyes. Set up your camera beforehand and check how you look and what's around you that can be seen. (You can do this by starting a new meeting on Zoom and checking the camera.)

- **Set up a light behind your computer facing you:** You want light to reflect on your face to help you look fresh and bright. If you don't have a light, or your light is behind you, you could look tired.

- **Prepare notes:** Put notes and your resume in eye shot for reference.

- **Dress professionally and look the part:** Just because you are online, it doesn't mean you should dress casually – wear what you would if you were meeting face to face. Solid colours are better for online and don't choose anything distracting. Smart casual is accepted during isolation; I would wear a nice dark jacket and plain shirt or similar.

  Men, make sure your facial hair is trimmed because everything is accentuated on the camera.

- **Record your interview:** This is a great way to look back and assess what you can do to improve for next time. If you don't know how to record, ensure you find out before the interview starts.

The process to getting the interview is just as important as the interview itself. Don't cut corners and think it is easy, because it isn't – but the end result makes the extra effort worthwhile.

CHAPTER THREE

No Sex in the Interview

How you perform at a job interview could have a major impact on your career prospects. No matter where you are in your career and how good your career record is to date, the interview remains an important step towards the fulfilment of your ambitions.

This chapter covers the most important questions I personally asked as a recruiter and what I heard my clients ask candidates over the years. These are questions you could be asked in your next interview, so I've also included tips on how you should respond. I also look at how women respond differently to men and why this could be holding them back in getting the role. With interviews, each gender is asked the same questions, so why should responses differ?

In every interview you should focus on what you have done and how you did it. Take preconceived blockers out of your head that prevent you from going into the interview as confident as you should be. Leave self-doubt at the door and keep sex out of the interview. Focus on you as an individual and what you can deliver.

See the interview process as an opportunity to meet someone new. At this interview, you will learn about what their company or division does and how you can help them, and achieve your personal career goals all at the same time.

Change your fear to excitement – into a 'can't wait to meet them!' approach. Remember, the interviewers know little to nothing about you, so here is your opportunity to shine.

Interview questions to expect

Let's run through some common interview questions that you should prepare for. Remember that your answers to these questions will leave a lasting impression with the interviewer.

Why have you applied for this role?

Your response to this question provides interviewers an insight into what motivated you to apply for the position. It's usually one of first questions asked for all role levels.

Here are some responses I have heard that a T10P would *never say:*

- 'It pays more.'
- 'I am not happy in my current role.'
- 'I heard I could work flexible hours.'
- 'I see it as a step towards something better.'
- 'I heard the company has a good parental leave policy.'

Keep comments about benefits and reasons for leaving until you are specifically asked about these areas. Hiring managers want to hear why you are interested in this role and what you will bring to the table.

Instead, tell them your career reason, such as:

- 'Managing a team has always been a goal of mine. I have the leadership skills that will take this team to its next level of success.'

- 'I am really passionate about xyz. I have the skills and capabilities to really add value to the role and the division.'

What interests you about our product or service?

Most hiring managers will ask this question, and this is where your research will come in handy. You need to know important details and show you made an effort to know what the company does.

You should feel confident to talk about the strengths and weaknesses of their products. Start with what you like and then discuss some of the areas that could be improved. Be diplomatic when you discuss negative features and suggest what could be done to improve them. They will also ask you about their competitors, so you should know who they are and what the differences are.

Can you tell me why you were only in xyz position for three months?

Everyone has a short-term role at some stage in their career and trying to cover it up is the wrong strategy. The truth is easier to remember. Be upfront and keep it simple. Don't be negative or blame anyone. For example:

- 'The role was made redundant due to company downsizing.'

- 'It wasn't the role described in the interview process and responsibilities moved in a different direction once I started.'

- 'I didn't align with the manager I reported to and thought it would be better for everyone to leave.'

If you had a negative experience with a manager, be diplomatic in your answer. We have all worked for someone who we did not respect or relate to. If you need to explain a short-term role, also run your answer past your mentor for their opinion and guidance. (See chapter 8 for more on mentors.)

What have you done that shows initiative in your career?

This is not a question about your achievements; instead, it's your chance to tell the interviewer about a time when you saw an opportunity for change within your company and took steps to implement that change, which resulted in a positive outcome. (You get bonus points if the change sat outside your normal job description.)

What are your weaknesses?

By far, this is the question that everyone hates to answer. The best way to answer is to look at those things you feel you need more training on.

- **Wrong way:** Saying something like, 'I am never on time' – is probably not a good idea.

- **Right way:** Instead you could say, 'I would like to improve the level of my technical skills in superannuation. I currently have xyz experience and would like to enhance this.' This will tell the interviewer what level of superannuation knowledge you have currently and what you need to develop.

What are your major achievements?

I have seen a clear difference to the way women answer this question versus the way men answer. As with their resumes, women's responses to this question usually don't meet the 'so what?' test. Why does this happen? Mainly because women haven't had mentors in the way that the guys have. I discuss this further in chapter 8.

Men tend to be able to talk about their achievements easily, sometimes even bringing them forward before they happen. Sorry guys, but this has been my experience. This usually occurs because men are confident that they will happen.

For example, when asked about their ability to meet sales targets, men will say something like:

'I am at 120 per cent of my target.'

But when I pressed, and asked them if they were at 120 per cent today, the answer would be more like:

'Not today; however, I am working on a big deal that will be completed in the next few months, and will take me to the 120 per cent of my target.'

If a woman were asked this question, she would be more likely to say something like:

'I am doing pretty well this year.'

When pressed for actual figures by asking, 'What does "pretty well" mean?', she would reply:

'As of today, I'm at 120 per cent of my target.'

With female candidates, I have always had to dig deeper to get them to verbalise their achievements. Women often use the word 'we' when referring to an achievement, even when it is their sole achievement, whereas men will claim the achievement as their sole achievement regardless of who else was involved.

Women have told me they felt they would come across as arrogant if they talked about their achievements. I would reply, 'If you talk about your achievements with passion and pride, it will never come across as arrogant. And if you don't talk about your achievements, who will?'

For both genders, it is important to make sure achievements are accurate.

> **Before any interview, have your achievements clear in your head. Know what the achievement was and how you did it.**

Make sure that if it is your achievement, say 'I'; if others were involved, bring 'we' in at the appropriate time. If it was your idea, say so; if others were involved, say what involvement they had.

Make sure achievement numbers are accurate. If you overstate an achievement, it will come out in reference checking.

REFLECTION

Have you ever wondered just how thorough reference checking is?

During the last assignment I did as a recruiter a few years ago, a candidate substantially overstated their achievements on their resume and in the interview.

The sales figures they overstated related to a role prior to the one they were currently in. I asked this candidate to provide details for the manager they reported to at that time; when I contacted the manager, they said the actual figures were a lot lower than what was stated.

Because the information was incorrect the candidate was not offered the role. My client was very disappointed because the candidate in question was the preferred candidate. The problem was that if they misrepresented this information, what would they do with company information in the future?

By being dishonest, the candidate missed a great opportunity and also damaged their brand.

The candidate probably thought the figures wouldn't be checked. During reference checking, expect companies to confirm details for at least the previous ten years. For more senior roles, checks could go back even further.

Behavioural interview questions

Once the basic questions are asked and satisfied, the interviewer will ask more detailed behavioural questions to get an idea of how you operate and your achievements. With behavioural type questions it is important to paint a picture. Your answers should cover the following:

- What was the situation?

- What action did you take?

- What was the result?

Don't over-explain situations; keep each response to around five minutes. You don't want to run out of time, resulting in the interviewer missing out on asking important questions.

Let's take a look at the top five behavioural questions I asked candidates for senior roles, along with some tips for what your responses should cover:

1. *When you started your current position, describe what your area of responsibility looked like. What does it look like now?*

   You want to be able to describe what your area of responsibility looked like the moment you started in the role, how you developed the position, and how it looks now. Focus on your achievements and any additional responsibilities you have added to your portfolio over time.

2. *Tell me about a time you had to change the direction of the organisation or team. What did you do and how did you set up the new direction?*

   Explain what was happening in your area that needed changing, and what steps you took to get the organisation to see that change was required. Once you got the approval for the changes, what did you do to set the new direction and what was the result?

3. *Tell me about a time when a staff member failed you. What did you do?*

   When speaking about staff, don't use names. Talk about the situation, what you needed to do to fix it and how it was resolved.

4. *Describe a situation where you successfully influenced a client or stakeholder using your technical expertise. How did you succeed?*

   This is where you have the opportunity to explain how you influenced stakeholders internally or external clients. It is an opportunity to describe a big win you had to get something over the line, and outline how you did it and the results.

5. *Tell me about a time when you had a significant challenge in delivering results. What was it and what did you do?*

   Every role has challenges. Demonstrate how you got through a tough time, how you showed resilience, how you encouraged others to come along and how you got to the other side successfully.

REFLECTION

How much thought have you put into your responses to behavioural questions? Can you keep your responses succinct and fresh?

I was interviewing for a marketing role at FEW a couple years ago and short-listed a candidate (let's call her Grace) who looked great on paper, presented professionally, and was confident.

On her resume, I didn't recognise one of the companies she had worked for, so I asked Grace what they did. Immediately Grace rolled her eyes. I said, 'Grace, why did you roll your eyes?' She replied, 'People ask me that question all the time, and then it takes me 20 minutes to explain and we run out of time. It's very annoying.'

I replied, 'Grace, I won't be offering you this role; however, if you like, I will spend the next 40 minutes coaching you on why – and what you could do next time to improve.' She seemed shocked, but accepted.

I said to Grace, 'You are a marketing person. This means you need to communicate clear messages to a market in one or two sentences; it should never take 20 minutes to explain what a company does.'

She explained that she had been to 11 first interviews with no call backs. I said to her that some of the answers she had provided in the interview sounded rehearsed, and that she had a tone of negativity. Interviewers don't care if you have been to several interviews, so you need to be positive at every interview.

I told her she exhibited confidence but needed to back her confidence by demonstrating with her skills and capabilities and showing passion for what she has done.

Grace was grateful for the coaching and said I was the first person to provide her with this kind of feedback. Another reason for mentors!

Interview reminders

You are being interviewed because the interviewer wants to hire someone, not because he or she wants to trip you up or embarrass you. During the interview, the interviewer will be searching out your strong and weak points, evaluating you on your qualifications, skills and intellectual qualities and probably probing deeply to determine your attitudes, aptitudes, stability, motivation and maturity. The following sections provide a guide to use for every interview.

Watch your tone

It is not just the words that come out of your mouth that matter during the interview – it is also how you say them. What is your tone? Do you sound passionate about what you are saying? Do your answers paint a picture for the interviewer? Are you expressing your interest with your eyes and facial expressions? Are you over-talking to the point that the interviewer is getting bored?

Candidates can also become interview weary if they go for a lot of interviews. You need to make sure that you treat every interview as if it's a first one, so you don't come across as over it, arrogant or indifferent. Interviewing is hard each time you go, so you need to psych yourself up as if you were going on stage to present to a new audience.

REFLECTION

Have you ever had several first interviews? Did you know why you didn't go forward? If a pattern is emerging in your interview success rate, you need to re-evaluate your approach.

A FEW member told me that she had an interview via Zoom. After the interview, the company told her she was unsuccessful.

When she asked for feedback, they said they felt she was not interested.

I met with her via Zoom to gauge her approach. She was very professional; however, she came across as more serious online. Her face looked overly serious when she was not smiling.

I said to her that she needed to make more of an effort to smile during interviews and to also say to the interviewer at the end how interested she was and why, to remove any doubt in their mind. I also highly recommended that she recorded her next meeting to self-assess herself and see where she could improve.

Know your audience

This is the part where you make sure that you go into the interview as a professional and are not overly familiar with the hiring manager. That doesn't mean you shouldn't try to form a relationship with them and break the ice, but ensure you keep it professional.

Don't assume that because the interviewer is male, they will want to talk about the football, or that women will like it when you comment on their shoes. Take sex completely out and focus on your capabilities and the role.

Remember to use the same kind of language and courtesies you would use if you were speaking to your next biggest client or a new stakeholder. Don't think that you need to mirror the interviewer – you be you. Keep it professional and focus on the role and what you can offer.

REFLECTION

Do you find yourself changing your language and approach, based on the sex and style of people interviewing you?

I was recruiting for a senior role that required a candidate to work with high-net-worth clients. Two good candidates were short-listed and had interviewed several times and with several stakeholders in the process. The role was Melbourne-based and the head of the division, from Sydney, came to Melbourne for the final interview.

The candidate who was the preferred choice with all the managers was very confident that he had it in the bag – and so was I. He had great experience with all the requirements for the role.

The divisional manager rang me after the interview and said he was not going forward with the preferred candidate. In shock, I asked why. He said, 'The interview was going well and I was suitably impressed; however, when we were finished, the candidate said, "Thanks, mate".'

I talked to the client about the Melbourne market, and how conditions in the area the candidate was interviewed for were not as formal as they were in Sydney. The client then said, 'I understand, Judith; however, him calling me "mate" shows he didn't know his audience, because I am not a "mate" person. I want someone who can read people and if he had done his research he would have known that'.

I couldn't argue with the client, because the candidate should have known his audience and that being too familiar – such as calling someone 'mate', or 'buddy' and anything like – is not a good idea. This candidate got to the final interview being professionally friendly, but then he took it one step too far, by calling the interviewer 'mate'.

Remember – keep your language professional at all times during the interview.

Tips for revenue generators

If you are a revenue generator, you should know exactly how you are tracking when you attend your interview. Do not use excuses such as the company doesn't provide you with up-to-date numbers. All good revenue generators know how much business they have brought in. Men and women aren't divided when it comes to who is a good revenue generator. Bringing business in the door is a skill that does not have a sex.

When interviewing for sales roles, most candidates present professionally and come across as confident. They often fall short, however, when describing their results.

Here are my top interview tips for revenue generators:

- Always quantify your achievements – for example, 'I am currently tracking at 80 per cent of my target and on track for 110 per cent by June'.

- If you are the highest performer in your team, mention that – for example, 'I am currently the highest performing BDM in the team'.

- If you are below target, highlight any reasons for this that are outside your control – for example, 'I am currently at 40 per cent of target due to economic circumstances, and all the team are tracking at 30 to 40 per cent'.

- Never make up figures or overstate achievements – you will always get caught out at reference checking time and it will damage your brand.

The interview is a two-way street

Regardless of what level you are interviewing for, the interview process is your chance to ascertain if the role is right for you. Don't take a role if you aren't interested in it, and make sure you know what you are getting yourself into.

Leaving a role after a short period – for example, because it wasn't what you thought it would be – will make your resume unstable if it happens too many times. To avoid this, be prepared to ask questions. Keep in mind that the questions should be asked in a conversational and not confrontational way.

Probing questions you might ask include the following:

- How has the division been tracking and what are the growth plans for the next year?

- What are your expectations in the first three to six months and what would you like me to have achieved by the end of the first year?

- Is there anything that isn't working that you want me to fix right away?

- Why do you like your job and what is the best part of working in this area? If you could change anything what would you change?

- What is your management style and how do you like your team to work with you?

If you require flexibility in the job, be sure to discuss this at the interview. This is not a gender issue; it is what you need as an individual to balance your work and outside commitments, so be clear about your requirements. You should discuss most of your flexibility requirements with the recruiter prior to the interview and then confirm these before accepting the role so there are no misunderstandings. For example:

- If travel is required, ask what will be required on a weekly or monthly basis so you understand the commitment.

- If you need to have flexibility around picking up children or carer responsibilities, make sure the company understands what you need.

Final tips

Here I've included some final do's and don'ts concerning the interview. First the 'do's':

- DO plan to arrive a few minutes early. Arriving late for a job interview is never excusable.

- DO greet the interviewer by his or her name if you are sure of the pronunciation. If you are not, ask them to repeat their name.

- DO greet with a smile, and shake hands if possible.

- DO be aware of your facial expressions and hand gestures, especially if interviewing online – expressions are often more pronounced on-screen.

- DO make sure to smile and show interest during the interview.

- DO mute your computer when you are not talking if you are in an online interview.

- DO look a prospective employer in the eye while you talk to him or her.

- DO follow the interviewer's lead but try to get the interviewer to describe the position and the duties to you early in the interview so that you can relate your background and skills to the position.

- DO make sure that you get your good points across to the interviewer in a factual, sincere manner. Keep in mind that you alone can sell yourself to an interviewer. Make the interviewer realise the need for you in their organisation.

■ DO always conduct yourself as if you are determined to get the job you are discussing. Never close the door on opportunity.

And now the 'don'ts':

■ DON'T answer questions with a simple 'yes' or 'no'. Explain whenever possible. Tell those things about yourself which relate to the position.

■ DON'T lie. Answer questions as truthfully, frankly and 'to the point' as possible.

■ DON'T ever make derogatory remarks about your present or former employers or companies.

■ DON'T 'over-answer' questions. Keep your answers succinct.

■ DON'T enquire about aspects such as salary, holidays, bonuses and retirement at the initial interview unless the employer brings the subject up.

Watch out for the deal breakers

During the course of an interview, the interviewer will be evaluating your negative factors as well as your positive attributes. Some of the negative factors frequently evaluated during the interview and which most often lead to rejection include the following:

■ Poor personal appearance – whatever your style, you can still incorporate a professional look.

■ Overbearing, overly aggressive or conceited tone – this comes across as a 'know it all' with a 'superiority complex'.

- Inability to express thoughts clearly.

- Use of slang or swear words.

- Lack of planning for career – this implies having no purpose or goals.

- Lack of interest and enthusiasm – this looks passive and indifferent.

- Lack of confidence or extreme nervousness – these are seen as negative, but can be turned around. If you find nerves are getting the better of you, and you're shaking or fumbling, be honest and tell the interviewer you are nervous because you really want to do well.

- Over-emphasis on money – this implies you're interested only in remuneration.

- Evasive answers – such as making excuses for unfavourable factors on record.

- Lack of tact, maturity or courtesy.

- Condemnation of past employers.

- Failure to look the interviewer in the eye.

- Lack of appreciation of the value of experience.

- Failure to ask questions about the job.

- Persistent attitude of 'what can you do for me?'

- Lack of preparation for the interview – including failing to get information about the company, which affects your ability to ask intelligent questions.

Ensure you remove any of these from your interview style if they are present. Again – if unsure, record yourself during an interview or seek advice from a mentor.

Closing the interview

If you are interested in the position, let the interviewer know and show them why you are interested. Ask the interviewer what the next steps are. If she or he offers the position to you, and you want it, accept on the spot. If you wish for some time to think it over, be courteous and tactful in asking for the time. Set a definite date when you can provide an answer.

Don't be too discouraged if no definite offer is made or specific salary discussed. The interviewer will probably want to communicate with their office first or interview more applicants before making a decision.

If you get the impression that the interview is not going well and that you have already been rejected, don't let your disappointment show. Once in a while an interviewer who is genuinely interested may seem to discourage you in order to test your reaction. They also may have something else on their mind that is distracting them, so don't take it personally. I had a lot of candidates call me after the interview thinking that they didn't do well, to then end up getting the job. Your perception is often not the reality when it comes to interviews.

You want to leave the hiring manager knowing three things:

1. You are interested in the job and the company (and why).

2. You are passionate and will fit into their team.

3. You have things to offer and will do a great job.

After the interview

After every interview T10Ps will send an email to the interviewer thanking them for their time and restating their interest. If they don't hear back by the agreed time, they will always follow up for a progress update. If they are unsuccessful in getting the role, they accept it with grace and dignity.

> **REFLECTION**
>
> No matter the result of an interview, don't give up.
>
> When I was recruiting, the short-list was usually two to three candidates. The final decision about who got the role was always the client's. Over the years, candidates who got angry about not getting the role and blamed everyone but themselves were never considered again for future roles. The candidates who accepted the decisions, and who were gracious in defeat, were always considered for future opportunities. Their reactions told me a lot about how they were as a person. Those candidates were mainly T10Ps and I would go out of my way to find them the right opportunity.
>
> If you didn't get the role and someone who you think is not as good as you did, don't immediately think it is discriminatory. Most of the reasons good candidates don't get the roles relate to how they performed at the interview. The ones who are successful in getting the role have several things in common – including that they follow all the interview tips I've included in this chapter. In my experience, the decision on who got the role was never based on a gender issue.

Don't give up. What you learnt in the first interview process will help you next time. Always take something from each process that you can learn from and ask the hiring manager what skills you would need to be the successful candidate next time. This is valuable information that makes the effort of applying worth it. Start putting in place training to improve the skills you need for next time.

CHAPTER FOUR

No Sex on Your First Day at Work

Arriving at work for your first day at a new job is your opportunity to make a great impression. It doesn't matter if this is your very first job or a new role in another division or company, and it certainly shouldn't matter what your gender is. This is your opportunity to take sex out of the equation and be you – the individual business-person you know you can be.

In this chapter, I give you tips to increase your chances for a successful induction when starting a new job. Don't take sex into work, and build your skills in speaking out when someone else tries to. Show your new boss you have the skills and capabilities to do the job and squash any gender stereotypes they may have.

First impressions count

Let's start with making a good first impression. The formal interviewing process may be over, but you are still being interviewed after you walk in the door because you are in your probationary period.

During your probation, the company can decide to let you go for any reason. Most junior roles have a three-month probation and senior roles can have a six- to twelve-month probation period.

From the moment you walk in the door, everything you say and do will be under the microscope, with feedback coming from every direction. Stakeholders, staff and clients will all have an opinion about you. If the opinion is negative, you could be having a performance meeting in your first few months.

REFLECTION

Do you consider the culture of your new workplace when making a good first impression? And how do you respond to feedback about the impression you're making?

At one of my first jobs, my boss pulled me aside and told me he had received feedback that I was aggressive. I very naïvely replied to him, 'Thanks! They think I'm assertive?'

He said, 'No Judith, they don't mean assertive. They think you are aggressive – you are too direct in your interactions with them'.

He told me that I needed to get to know the staff and be more conversational. He highlighted I was bringing in the culture of my old company and not getting to know their culture, which was very different.

I was very thankful for his counsel and knew he had my best interest at heart. Had he not been prepared to give me that advice, I would not have made it through my probation period. I wonder how many managers today would be prepared to tell female employees that they are being aggressive.

When I have told this story at presentations, someone will always raise their hand and say, 'He only told you that because you are a woman'. I reply every time in a similar way: 'No, I was directional in my approach, which was perceived as aggressive and it had nothing to do with my gender'. The mistake I made was not taking the time to understand the new culture and immediately thinking the new company would be the same as my old company.

Every workplace is different, with its own unique culture. Take some time in any new job to get a feel for this culture and your impression of the people in it, as well as considering the impression you're making.

I didn't walk into my first job or any job thereafter and think, *I'm a female. People will discriminate against me and I will not be promoted. Guys will hit on me and make rude remarks. I will be treated differently.*

I'm not saying this kind of bad behaviour doesn't happen in workplaces. However, it never crossed my mind that I would be starting on the back foot because of my gender. I was competitive and wanted to prove my worth – not because I was a girl and had something to prove, but because I wanted to get ahead, and I knew I was just as capable as anyone else.

Take gender out of the equation and focus on the job.

Remember – speak up about the barriers that do exist, but don't create them when they don't. If you go into an environment with a preconceived idea, it can affect how you see the culture and how you respond (or fail to respond).

When I was told I was aggressive (as I outlined in the previous Reflection), the feedback was in relation to an unwanted style I was exhibiting in a new culture that operated differently. Perhaps being female accelerated their perception and made them more attuned to it; however, I didn't see it that way at the time and appreciated the feedback.

Interestingly, the complaints about my aggressive behaviour were made by two of the female staff. Were they being discriminatory? Or were they similar to the mean girls at school and being competitive with me and not accepting me into their group? (See the section 'Back to school', later in this chapter, for more on this.)

I could have taken offence and said it was because of my gender, but I didn't, because what my boss was saying to me was logical. I accepted the critique and got on with doing the best job I could.

Do women respond differently to situations than men?

If you take critique and feedback with your sex in mind and think everything a manager tells you is because of your gender, you can let your defensiveness block the reality of the situation. It is hard for people to provide constructive feedback, and I don't know too many people who love to criticise others.

When starting a new job, you will make mistakes. Listen to what is being said and accept the feedback as genuine. Your gut instinct will often tell you if it is discriminatory and if you have doubts, ask someone you respect and trust. Starting any new role is stressful. Don't take things personally or over-analyse. Don't dwell on an exchange for weeks and let tension build up; speak to someone and get advice.

Misconceptions are the cause of a lot of problems at work.

I have seen people leave good jobs, fire good people, make terrible business decisions, and damage the brand of others because they perceived a situation incorrectly and didn't ask questions.

Speak up or lose out

Traditionally, boys are encouraged to speak up and take charge. Girls are told they are bossy if they speak up and this is seen as a negative. So it's understandable that these ideas have filtered through into the work environment.

I was lucky to have been brought up to speak up or lose out. However, I have seen young women starting out in their careers being quiet and not speaking up if they see issues. They also tend to say that something is the way it is, even when it isn't or doesn't have to be, so they don't rock the boat.

Have you ever been afraid to ask a question or speak up in the early days on the job because you didn't think you should? Take the sex out of work and be you. All the skills you need to get from A to B, and to become part of the T10Ps, are gender neutral. You can learn these skills if you take the blockers away. Be confident from your first day at a new job – as both men and women should be – because those first impressions count.

REFLECTION

Have you ever been bothered by something, but not spoken up about it? Or, when you did speak up about something, did you discover the situation wasn't how you'd perceived it to be?

Last year at one of the FEW conferences, a young woman approached me and asked if I could tell her if she was being discriminated against. She had been working as a business development consultant with a large financial institution for about four months. To put this in context, a business development consultant is the first step to being a business development manager (BDM). She would be in training for the higher-level role of BDM, although in both roles you manage a portfolio of clients.

She said she had been given all the clients that none of the current BDMs in her team wanted, and so wondered if she was being discriminated against. She even said she was wondering if she should leave.

I told her the company she was with was a great company and, from my experience with them, very committed to diversity. And I went on to explain that it was normal for a company to give new staff lower risk clients to see how they go first, before they are handed the good clients. She was just the new kid on the block.

I highlighted that if other new and junior staff members were given good clients and she was being singled out and given low-risk clients, that would be discrimination. However, that was not the case in her situation. I said I was really happy that she discussed the situation with someone, instead of keeping it inside.

When people don't speak up, discrimination gets accepted. However, in this case, this woman's mistaken perception of the situation concerned me. I felt somewhere down the line, she must have been influenced by information that made her defensive. Is every new graduate coming into the work environment going to think situations they don't understand have to do with discrimination? I felt my conversation with her set things straight and made a difference, but what about the next time?

This was also an example of how companies could have a better induction process, and ensure they explain the role in more detail to the new entrant. If her boss had told her why she was getting the low-risk clients, things would likely have been different in her eyes.

Can you think of any situations in your current or previous workplaces that could have been explained better – either to you, or to other new recruits?

Back to school

I mentioned those mean girls from school earlier in this chapter. But they're not the only ones in the workplace who haven't left childish behaviours behind. When you think about it, workplaces are like schools for grown-ups. And what we learnt during our school years is often carried into the work environment. So let's go back to school and think about how the different relationships and hierarchies can still apply today.

The minute we walk into a new role, we will start to see the old schoolyard.

The main players include:

- **The principal: the CEO – the one who calls all the shots.**
  Depending on your level, you may not even get to see this person. If they do ask you to come to their office, do you immediately think you have done something wrong?

- **The teachers: the managers – some you like and some you don't.**
  Over the years, some will be inspirational mentors; some will make your life miserable.

- **The student body: your colleagues and stakeholders.**
  You will form lifelong friendships with some people in this group, and some will help you get what you want. Some will best be forgotten.

- **The bullies: competitive colleagues who want your job and seek to undermine you.**
  Learning how to stand up for yourself will give you an edge in turning the school bully into a thing of the past.

- **The teacher's pet: the co-worker who is perceived by the boss to be the best thing since sliced bread.**

  Don't upset the teacher's pet, because they have the ear of the teacher.

- **The guru: someone always blowing their own horn about how great they are.**

  Before you classify someone as a guru, make sure they have the track record to back it up. Don't follow mediocre people who fool others into believing they are great; get the facts.

- **The geeks: the really smart people who can help you with your work if you let them.**

  Who doesn't need help or advice at some stage? Surround yourself with people you can learn from!

- **The mean girls and mean boys: they will not let you into their clique, and they laugh at you and talk behind your back.**

  These people are very similar to the bullies, but operate in a pack. Don't buy in to office gossip and remember most things you say will be repeated at some stage.

- **The janitors: the people who clean up the mess.**

  Are you the person who always has to clean up the mess? I suggest you start speaking to the smart people on how to solve that problem.

Over the years, I have seen schoolyard behaviour replicated within major organisations and even my own businesses, and unfortunately sometimes people never grow up.

Think about how sex/gender bias played a part when you were in school. Did you bring any of those behaviours or biases into the workplace?

Let's look at some of the skills you can learn to get yourself out of the schoolyard and back into the adult world as a professional businessperson.

Don't 'levelise'

Okay, I may have made up a word, but let me explain. 'Levelising' is when you treat someone differently because of their level in the business. It's when you think someone is more, or less, important than someone else based on their role, and treat them accordingly.

Levelising could also give a discriminatory impression. You could be seen as sexist or racist because you are being dismissive of someone you feel is at a lower level than you.

You could also unconsciously be levelising someone who is in your team (at the same level as you) and not realising you are damaging a relationship.

REFLECTION

Are you guilty of levelising? Do you feel able to speak up when you see it?

Early in my career, I had to see a client with a male member of my team who was at the same level as me. When we got to the client's office, he said in front of the client, 'Judith will take the notes'.

I didn't say anything in front of the client; however, the second we got back to our office, I told him that I did not like the idea of taking the notes and giving the impression that I was his assistant. He apologised and I got him to agree that, for every appointment we attended together, one person would open the meeting and one would close the meeting and notes would be taken by the person who was not talking. That way the client would see us as equal.

> How do you treat others? Pay attention to how you are communicating to others because you may be levelising – even when you think you're not. The majority of people will not speak out as I did, and will harbour resentment for how you are treating them.

You can take your first step to avoiding levelising on your first day in a new job. Take the time to introduce yourself to the receptionist and administration staff. Many people make the (big) mistake of not developing good relationships with staff in lower level positions. Everyone has a role to play in building a successful business, and you should treat everyone equally, with respect. Every relationship is important, and it is much better to have allies than enemies; you never know when your supporters will help you behind the scenes.

Creating enemies will have the opposite effect. If you think the receptionist or office staff are just there for your service, think again. Treating people like servants will backfire on you in the long run. People have long memories, and your paths are highly likely to cross again.

Once negative feedback is given about you to a manager, getting the next role reporting to that person will be very hard.

People have long memories when it comes to negative feedback. A rude comment you made ten years ago could come back to bite you when you don't expect it.

People respond positively to respect and kindness, and will remember you in a positive way if this is how you treat them.

Managers often ask their trusted people what they think of a new staff member during their early days in the role. It's much better if your manager hears, 'Oh, she's great!' rather than, 'Yeah, she's okay'.

Remember the schoolyard examples I covered previously? When you enter a new role or new company, you need to sort out the characters and start assessing the situation from day one.

When you decide who is important and who isn't and treat them accordingly, you make a fundamental mistake. The T10Ps know that everyone is an important stakeholder.

Communicate with common courtesies

Remember the common courtesies such as 'hello', 'please' and 'thank you'? This may sound funny, but because common courtesies are dying in the workplace, you will immediately stand out if you practise them. The T10Ps, no matter their gender, never forget the common courtesies.

People tell me all the time that their boss never says hello when they come into the office in the morning. This seems unbelievable to me, but maybe you've also experienced this. While the complaints are about both men and women bosses, the resulting perceptions are different. When a female boss doesn't say hello, this is often perceived as a personality issue – such as *she's a b***h*. When a male boss is at fault, he is often perceived as being arrogant. One is undoubtedly worse than the other, but both perceptions are not good.

Don't think that by displaying the common courtesies you will be seen as weak. Perhaps this is the thought process for both women and men who have been told that in order to be a leader, you need to be tough and unapproachable. That is not leadership: that is arrogance and T10Ps are not arrogant.

> **Forget what you have learnt in the past about what you should or shouldn't do and just focus on what T10Ps do as good leaders. It's not a gender trait; it's a leadership trait.**

T10Ps (men and women) know that it is just as important to develop relationships with their staff as it is with the people they report to. Addressing staff in the morning is just part of a T10P's routine.

Whether or not you are the boss or one of the team, take a leadership approach the minute you enter your new role. Be the person who sets the example. Saying hello to people in the office when you arrive for the day might sound basic and may feel a little uncomfortable, but it will make a big difference for such little effort. As a leader (or potential leader), you need to step out of your comfort zone and communicate. This will leave a good impression and people will start to remember you, in a good way.

Sometimes I wonder whether we are so locked into technology that we are forgetting to connect with the people who are in front of us and part of our team.

Don't be one of these people. Don't think that human connection is old school. The T10Ps know that technology will never replace real relationships. They know that developing relationships face to face is actually a leadership quality.

I have met so many good connections in the elevator at work. I always say hello or smile as I enter into the elevator. Try this yourself – start with 'Good morning' and see what happens. Don't think that because you are a woman, you shouldn't say hello to a man, or if you are a man, you shouldn't say hello to a woman. If you think this way, you could be cutting out 50 per cent of a network. What have you got to lose? It might be your opportunity to connect with someone who will be your next boss or client.

If you are at a more junior level, find the courage to look people in the eye and make a connection. If someone is not acknowledging you, be the one who starts the process. If they don't respond, this is a reflection on them – not you.

Practising common courtesies is one of the easiest things you can do to meet new connections, and build good relationships with staff, stakeholders and clients. This approach is not about gender; it's just good leadership.

REFLECTION

Do you still remember common courtesies and to be polite to all members of your team? Or do you think these courtesies only apply to certain people?

When I worked in banking, I encountered two clients who were brokers dealing with high-net-worth clients.

One broker was arrogant and thought all his deals should be processed by the settlements team as first priority. He would jump up and down if his deals weren't settled quickly enough and criticise staff to their manager.

The other broker was nice, polite and respectful to the settlements team. He would thank them for their work and occasionally bring them cupcakes on a Friday.

Fridays were important days, because both brokers wanted to finalise their clients' loans before the weekend.

One day, I noticed that the settlements team put all the nice broker's files on the top of the pile, to ensure settlement would occur on Friday. Often the arrogant broker would have to wait until Monday, whereas the settlements team would go the extra mile for the nice broker – even working through lunch if needed.

The flow-on effect of this was that the nice broker had a better relationship with his clients because he could deliver the settlement of their loan on the day he promised.

Who do you rely on in your organisation? How are you treating them? If you were nicer, what impact would that have on the way they perceive you and the delivery of your job?

Building on those good first impressions

First impressions count, but that's just the beginning. As you settle into your first 12 months at your new job, you need to continue to build relationships and improve communication with your boss, colleagues and stakeholders. In the following sections, I offer some tips in these and other areas that all T10Ps know to focus on.

Ask your new boss what their expectations are

Why are so many people – no matter their gender – afraid to ask the hard questions? If you fall into this category, is it because you feel that you will come across in a certain way? Or are you afraid of the answers?

Your company hired you to fulfil a role. You need to know exactly what is expected to be successful in that role.

No doubt you discussed expectations in the interview, but you are in the job now and it is important to clarify the detail. Even if you have a position description, these are often generic and so can't be relied on. You should ask for more information.

I have found women tend not to ask direct questions about salary packages but ask for more details on the job and expectations. Men tend to negotiate every dollar and benefit, and don't worry as much about the job details. I think both of these aspects are important, and if you want to be a T10P you must be brave enough to seek clarity in both areas.

Confirm expectations upfront to prevent issues later.

Don't leave job responsibilities or the salary package subject to interpretation. Lack of communication causes misunderstandings and gets people in trouble. If misinterpretations mean you haven't achieved certain requirements by the end of your probation period, it is too late. In addition, not clarifying your bonus structure upfront could be the cause of heated discussions in the future.

Ask your boss in the first week for a sit-down meeting and go over the following:

- What needs to be achieved in the first 3, 6 and 12 months? If you don't understand their answers, ask questions for verification. (If you are in a sales role, you need specific targets, budgets and deadlines.)

- What budget and resources are available to meet these targets?

- Should you be aware of any current issues?

- How would your boss like you to communicate with them – via email, in person at a regular meeting or ad hoc as required?

- If you require flexibility because of external commitments such as family, make sure this has been agreed to and everyone is on the same page. Remember to take gender out of the conversation. This is what you need as an individual to balance your work and outside commitments. Don't apologise or make excuses; be clear on what you already discussed at the interview stage and make sure nothing has changed.

After this meeting, send an email to your boss, thanking them for their time and confirming everything you agreed to in writing. Keep this email in a folder on your desktop for easy access.

If your boss's expectations are unrealistic, this is the time to discuss it – not 6 or 12 months later when it is too late.

Remember the pre-nup? This exists for a reason. After the honeymoon, things can change and if you haven't set the rules of engagement, the 'war of the roses' can occur.

REFLECTION

Think back to your first few weeks in previous roles. Could communication between you and your boss have been better?

Several years ago, I placed a general manager who rang me after one month in the role and said he was not happy. The role was not what he thought, and he was questioning why he had taken it. When I asked him why he felt that way, he said it was because the managing director hadn't bothered to see how he was going, and he didn't know if he was on the right track.

I then contacted the MD and asked him how he thought his new hire was going - to which he replied, 'Great! I haven't had to worry about him, and he has hit the ground running'.

I replied, 'You may like to touch base with him, because during the probationary period new hires need to know they are on the right track. This is a sensitive time when candidates can still decide to leave organisations if they are not settling in'. He promised he would call him that day.

After a week, I followed up the new general manager, who let me know he'd had the meeting with the managing director. He was so happy, and wondered why he had been worried about the role or his performance. They mapped out a plan for the following months, and communication flowed well from then on.

Had they had a meeting upfront and set expectations, none of this would have happened. This situation taught me a lesson about ensuring that communication flows with new hires and, from that time onwards, I always briefed the candidate and the client on how they should communicate information in the first year.

Regardless of how long you've been in a role, think about how well communication is flowing and, if needed, what you could do to improve it.

Keep it positive

People notice new employees and any behaviour from them – positive or negative – is often amplified. Make sure you have a positive attitude, and don't be drawn into office politics. Every organisation has people who see the new person as an opportunity to build an alliance (think *Survivor*). You could be starting a role in a team where major changes are happening, and some people may not be happy about it – but it's never a good idea to take sides or become your colleagues' sounding board. Stay out of the gossip and don't respond to negative comments or opinions.

If you feel it is necessary to respond, just say something like, 'That has not been my experience' or 'I haven't been here long enough to form an opinion'.

Negative colleagues can often twist a comment you make innocently and repeat it to others, which could damage your personal brand. (See the following chapter for more on your personal brand.) Don't say anything that may come back to bite you.

Keep focused on no sex at work. No matter their gender, T10Ps focus on the job they have to do – not on office politics or office gossip.

Get to know who is who

Make an effort to introduce yourself to colleagues and stakeholders. Don't wait for introductions – others might be waiting for you to make the first move, so take the initiative.

Take gender out of your head when you are getting to know who is who in the new company or division. Bringing sex to work limits your network. This applies whether you're a woman worried that approaching a male colleague will be seen as flirting, or a man worried that approaching a female colleague will be seen as harassment. Keep it professional and you won't have a problem, regardless of your gender. Remember what I said about saying hello when you get in the elevator – no matter what your gender!

Most of the senior people I have met when I was coming up the ladder in my career were men. For me, saying hello or having conversations had everything to do with just getting to know who was who. Don't put something in front of you that may or may not be there.

Use LinkedIn to connect with colleagues and stakeholders

When taking on any new role, use LinkedIn to your advantage. Search the platform using your company name and research which stakeholders you should meet from your new company or division. Again – if you stop yourself from connecting because of sex differences and stereotypes, you immediately limit your network and potentially miss out on meeting great contacts.

When you send your connection request, include in your message that you are a new employee with the company or division, what you do, and that you would like to connect with them.

Here are some further tips when connecting through LinkedIn:

- Connect with people one to two levels up from your position or colleague level, and also consider other levels where you are a direct stakeholder to their business.

- Don't forget to connect with the lower levels – they could be the next person you hire in your team.

- If you are really brave, go for connections with even higher levels and just say to yourself, 'What have I got to lose?' That's what I (and the T10Ps) would do!

Another tactic from the T10Ps is having a stakeholder management plan. On this, you include the names of those people you have connected with and who you feel you should meet. Once you've connected with a contact, reach out and suggest a coffee meeting. You need to have a reason to meet, but this could be as simple as you being interested in their area and wanting to tell them about yours.

If you don't hear back from this contact, don't take it personally because some senior people don't manage their own LinkedIn page. Keep in mind that the ones who do accept could be a great connection in the future.

Don't live in the past

Nothing is more annoying than someone saying something like, 'We used to do it like this at XYZ company' or 'At XYZ company we had this or that'.

Your new colleagues don't care what you did at XYZ company!

Don't compare unless they ask. Making comments like these comes across as if you are still tied to your old company or division and not engaging with the new. Get on the bus with the new company.

Take the time to understand your role and the culture you are going into. Clarify expectations so you know what you need to achieve. Align with people who are positive and don't levelise. Be mindful of the impression that you are giving.

With any new job, you will need more time to learn things and will work harder in the early months. You will doubt if you are good enough and if you made the right decision. It takes at least 6 to 12 months to settle into a new job, so give yourself time. Take sex at work out of the equation and focus on business skills that will help you succeed in the new role and thereafter.

CHAPTER FIVE

No Sex in Public

Be mindful of your exterior brand – what the public sees will be lasting.

How you present yourself to your colleagues or clients – whether in person, online or on stage doing a presentation – affects your career. How do you want people to see you? As an impressive professional, or as a stereotype you think society has labelled you as, which is nothing like the real you?

> **REFLECTION**
>
> How do you feel about your public brand? Do you work on it? Or do you feel you shouldn't have to?
>
> I once did a presentation to final-year university students about how to put their best foot forward in an interview and present professionally. After I had gone over the basics of what to wear and how to present, someone in the audience raised their hand.
>
> She said in a very abrupt and determined voice, 'If they don't like the way I look, that is their problem'.

I replied, 'Yes, that is probably true; however, once you have had 30 interviews and just as many rejections, it becomes your problem'.

Be honest with yourself. Are your own beliefs and attitudes preventing you from presenting yourself in the best way possible? Are you putting limitations on yourself because of an outdated society perception?

Do you want to be a T10P or one of the crowd?

Presentation is everything

Remember when I said my grandmother wasn't particularly attractive? She didn't need to be the most beautiful person in the room because she was confident in herself. When she spoke, people listened. How did she do it?

She took pride in her presentation. She knew her brain was her biggest asset, but that she still needed to present herself well to be taken seriously. She was short, but size didn't limit her, and in her mind she didn't need to be tall in stature to be noticed. She was heavy, but that didn't stop her from being stylish. She was a woman and proud of it, and her sex was not a barrier to success.

You could have purple hair and love to wear what is considered totally outside the box of normal business attire, but if you are smartly presented and keep it simple, you can own your individual style in a professional way.

I have been to meetings with people in T-shirts and jeans who presented better than the person next to them in the wrinkled suit who looked like they'd had a hard night. Sex does not discriminate when it comes to presentation; wrinkled clothes are not an option for any T10P, no matter their gender.

If your goal is to be a leader, lead by example. Just because everyone else in your area is sloppy, that doesn't mean you should be.

Presentation on a budget

It might surprise you to learn that looking professional does not need to cost a lot of money. My advice: be smart with how you spend your hard-earned money and don't get caught up in fads and brands.

My mother taught me that money does not buy style or class. She told me to shop for quality – and that doesn't mean it needs a brand name with a big price tag.

She said to buy pieces that will last, and warned me against filling my closet with junk that I would never wear.

Women, in particular, are overcharged for clothing all the time. When you compare the prices to what men pay for similar items, you notice a huge difference. Go figure that men make more money and pay less for their clothes. It does my head in!

> **When I interviewed candidates (both women and men), I didn't know if they wore a designer suit. All I knew was whether or not they looked professional.**

REFLECTION

How complicated do you make your business attire?

If men can get away with wearing a blue or a black suit and that is acceptable (as long as it is tidy and professional), who is judging women for not wearing designer clothes, shoes and handbags?

Most of the men I know would not have a clue about what is designer and what isn't. So are we women putting this pressure on ourselves? As women, are we spending money on items that aren't worth it and that could be better spent elsewhere? Are women buying for themselves, or to impress others?

Think about how you can change the landscape to remove the rules on what each gender should wear in the workplace. How can you help eliminate the sex division, so that when people walk into your workplace they are seen as an individual, not a gender?

Five tips for professional presentation

Here are some quick tips on looking professional without blowing your budget:

1. If you are working in professional services, invest in a range of pieces that are interchangeable. For example, choose clothes that can interchange with different accessories, and shirts or blouses that can interchange with different suits. Keep the core wardrobe items simple.

2. Make sure your clothes fit well and are not wrinkled. Pay attention to personal grooming. Shoes and handbags or satchels should be good quality and not worn out. People do look from head to toe.

3. Make sure you're aware of the dress code for your organisation. Have a style that fits in with the company culture but also makes you feel comfortable. Look at what the CEO of the company and the leadership team are wearing – this is always a good benchmark to follow.

4. If you can afford it, enlist a stylist to help sort out your wardrobe. This may be an expensive upfront cost, but in the long term you will save. A fresh eye will be able to look at you and give you constructive feedback without worrying about hurting your feelings. I have seen stylists transform people to the best version of themselves.

5. If you are unsure how you are presenting yourself, ask someone you trust and who is not afraid to give you a critique.

What are you portraying online?

Given how quick we can get information these days, it is highly likely that before you even start a job, people have checked you out. They'll have googled your name and looked at your LinkedIn profile and other social media.

What are you showing them? Would you hire you, based on the content about you that is available online?

The image you portray, especially on LinkedIn, is the impression other people will have of you – are you really putting your best foot forward?

REFLECTION

You need to consider all aspects of your online presence. For example, what does something as supposedly simple as your profile picture on platforms such as LinkedIn say about you?

In a keynote presentation I do about the T10Ps, I use several real-life examples of people on LinkedIn, showing these on a large screen for the audience to see.

One example I use is a woman from overseas who works for a bank. I put her profile on the screen and ask the audience what their first impression is.

The audience will stare at the screen for a few moments and then several people will raise their hands and comment that while she is well presented, where she is standing is not good. The woman has had her picture taken in her home with the kitchen as the backdrop.

I point out to the audience that we have been trying to squash the stereotype that a woman's place is in the kitchen for years, so standing in front of a kitchen for your picture is not a good look.

In another example, I show a financial analyst who is also very well presented. In his case, he is standing in front of a racecourse.

I point out to the audience that his credibility will be in question because he hasn't got the sense to know that standing in front of the racecourse as a credit person will do damage to his brand and the company he works for.

How are you presenting yourself to the world? Are you contributing to the stereotype society has of women or men? Or are you keeping sex out of your profile so people can focus on you as an individual professional?

Making an impression before your first impression

Making an impression online is similar to making an impression in person. It used to be said that we have five minutes to make a good first impression. But now, before people even meet you, they will check you out and form an impression of you in about 30 seconds based on your online profile.

Before you hit post, think about how others will perceive you in the future and whether that is the image you want to portray. This applies to anything you're posting online – whether on LinkedIn or any other social platform. Even posts that are completely unrelated to your working life are potentially visible to your boss and colleagues. Make sure your friends don't post pictures of you that you don't approve of, because this is also part of your digital footprint.

People looking you up online will also see if you have any connections in common – again, on LinkedIn, but on other platforms as well. They may ask these connections about you if you are a stakeholder or if you are applying for a job with them. This is when old conflicts could come back to bite you when you least expect it.

Focusing on your LinkedIn profile

Here are three easy steps to make sure you have a great LinkedIn profile that protects your exterior brand:

1. **Have a good profile picture.**

   You don't have to spend money on a photographer – you can just ask someone in your office or family to take a shot of you in work-appropriate clothes. Make sure you are standing in front of an appropriate backdrop – no kitchens or racecourses! Don't put pictures of you at a social event with the bridesmaid dress on or a drink in your hand. And no selfies please! Getting a good shot has become a lot easier with all the things we can now do on our smart phones.

   Also include a background photo that makes your picture stand out. Putting in a background image that is your company logo or something that represents you will make you stand out from the crowd. I have seen graphics, pictures of people speaking at events or just a solid colour used for the background image. Whatever you choose, get a second opinion from someone you trust when you have updated your LinkedIn photos. And for some inspiration, have a look at my LinkedIn profile at www.linkedin.com/in/judith-beck-6097234.

2. **Have a good summary.**

   Keep your summary brief and highlight what you are passionate about. For example, if you are a marketing person you could say something similar to Anna Siassios, who worked for me at FEW:

About

I am a marketing professional and business leader. I lead and develop an internal team to support the following areas: marketing, communications and business planning.

Together with the CEO, I make strategic decisions that enhance operations, ensuring the company's growth and performance.

I am a driven and qualified marketing manager who takes pride in delivering high-quality end-to-end marketing initiatives within budget and time constraints.

If I were to put my recruiter hat back on and was looking at Anna's profile, I would have a great snapshot of what she does. She also shows passion in how she delivers her message.

You want your stakeholders and clients to get an idea about who you are and what you are passionate about from your summary. If you don't take the time to build a good profile, people will assume things about you that may not be correct.

3. **Remember that LinkedIn is not your resume.**

Once you have written your summary, the next part is simple: list your employment history with the current employer first. If your summary didn't cover what you do within your current organisation, then state it under your current role.

Don't overstate what you did for each role – keep it simple and remember this is just a snapshot of your employment history. Think of your profile as being similar to an electronic business card that everyone can see.

Public speaking and presentations – keep sex out of it

You also build your public brand through your public speaking and presentations. Do you relate to any of these?

- You have been asked to give a presentation to the leadership team or at an industry conference and you are terrified because you hate getting up in front of people more than anything. The audience is mainly men and that also makes you uncomfortable.

- You are convinced that you are an introvert and public speaking isn't your strength.

- You feel a rush when you get onstage and find yourself speaking faster than normal, diverting from the slides or over-talking.

- Your last presentation bombed and now you are more nervous than ever to do it again.

I can relate to the last two bullet points in particular, and have experienced these at different times in my career.

Here, I share with you what I do now to overcome nerves while presenting, and to make sure the presentation is a success and the audience is happy.

I could write a whole book about public speaking and many people have, so I recommend that you also read *TED Talks: The official TED guide to public speaking* by Chris Anderson, Head of TED. It is easy to read with lots of good examples.

REFLECTION

How do you approach public speaking? Do you try to avoid it or find yourself underprepared?

When I ran my executive search business, I never needed to deliver presentations to large groups of people. I was very comfortable speaking in front of small groups and clients, but I hadn't experienced presenting to groups of 200 plus.

Around six years ago when FEW was in its second year, I was asked to do a presentation to over 250 people at NAB. I organised for a friend of mine – Vanessa Bennett, CEO of Next Evolution Performance – to also present. Vanessa is one of the most skilled presenters I have ever seen. Fortunately for me, I went on stage before Vanessa.

I did all the things I now tell people not to do. I hid behind the podium, I had copious notes which I read from, I'd prepared too many slides, I didn't practise enough before the day, and I didn't psych myself up before going on.

When it was Vanessa's time to speak, I saw what a great presenter does. From memory, she didn't even get up on the stage, but instead stood in front of the crowd so she was on their level. She had no notes and only a few slides, but she hardly looked at them. It was more like a performance than a presentation, and everyone was glued to her every word. *Thank god I didn't speak after her!* I thought.

I said to Vanessa after the presentation that I felt I had done a terrible job – and that she had been great. She said to me, 'Judith, I have done this presentation a hundred times. After a while you will know your presentation word for word – and if you forget something, no-one else will know because it is your presentation'.

The experience I had with Vanessa was an eye-opener. I knew if I was going to be comfortable getting up in front of a large audience, I needed to make some changes.

The fear people experience when they must do a presentation is so common – and it can make some people do just about anything to get out of it. Why are we so worried about getting up in front of people and talking about things we are experts in? I understand why people fear the spur of the moment, 'tell me about yourself' type of presentation where you are put on the spot. Everyone feels uncomfortable when this happens and they are unprepared. But when you know you must do a presentation and you have been asked because you are the expert, what is the big deal – right?

It is a big deal for most of us and will affect us all at some stage. Just know that everyone goes through this kind of anxiety at some point during their career and, no matter how confident someone is, very few will nail a presentation the first time they do it. Whether you are presenting to 10 or 1000 people, you can do a few things to help prepare yourself and ease your anxiety before and during the presentation. I'll get to those tips shortly – but first a quick look at sex in presentations.

Are men or women better at giving presentations?

Being a good speaker is not about sex – think about all the great actors who are women. Presenting is like acting with your own script.

The difference I have noticed is that men have more mentors in their corner who are more likely to help them with their first presentation.

Women also tend to feel more judged because they are still in the minority when it comes to speaking and any minority will feel like they are under the spotlight. They tend to doubt their abilities and worry more about what people will think. This doubt is unwarranted, because some of the best speakers I have seen are women. Get your script right, and present like it's a performance.

Tips for every presentation

Here are the tips I would like to share with you that help me every time I do a presentation:

- **Keep sex out of it:** When I get in front of people, I don't think of myself as a woman delivering a presentation. I think of myself as an expert delivering information to people who are there to learn.

- **Enjoy the experience:** Immediately change your mindset from dreading the idea of presenting to being excited. Once I started doing this, it changed the way I looked at doing presentations and my stress levels went down. I think about the presentation as, 'This will be fun, and I can't wait to meet everyone and share my information'. I also tell myself to be myself and to get as much out of the experience as I am putting in.

- **Remember the why:** You have been asked to do a presentation because someone wants to hear about your experience or the topic that you are an expert in. So, tell them as if you were in a group of friends, telling a story about an experience or educating them about something you are good at.

- **Be prepared:** Even though it is your story or your topic, you still need to be prepared.
  - If you are telling a story, keep the sequence in line – don't divert and start talking about something else. You will get confused on where you are at in the presentation and run the risk of repeating something you already said.
  - If you are doing a technical presentation, make sure your facts are correct. Tell the audience you will take questions at the end, so you don't get interrupted during the presentation.

- **Practise:** Practise your presentation several times and say it out loud. We all think we are great singers in our head, but when we sing out loud it is a whole different story. Listen to you own voice out loud and see if that joke you think is hilarious sounds as funny when you hear it.

- **Show up early:** This is one of the best tips I could give, and I strongly suggest doing this for all presentations (even for internal boardroom presentations). I find showing up early and talking to people as they arrive very effective because then when I start my presentation, several friendly faces are already in the audience and I focus my eye contact on them.

- **Break the ice and set any rules of engagement:** An opening thought-provoking question to the audience is always a great way to get the presentation going and the audience involved. If you don't want questions during the presentation, make sure you tell the audience that you will open for questions at the end.

- **Limit your slides:** I only use slides to keep my thoughts in sequence. I am definitely one of those people who can get diverted and go off script and then forget what I just said. Depending on the presentation I am doing, I have from five to eight slides with a relevant picture and very few words. This keeps my memory on track.

- **Step away from the podium:** If you really want to connect to your audience, step out from behind the podium. The podium becomes a barrier between you and the audience. Take the barrier away and, even though your mind will tell you that you need it, you will come across more confident if you are out in front. I have never seen a TED Talk presenter with a podium.

- **Don't tell jokes:** Being funny in a natural way is great; however, I have seen too many presenters tell a joke that they think the audience will find funny and all it does is alienate them. For example, assuming an audience of women is going to think the way you do because you are also a woman is often misguided. Keep gender, religion, politics and race out of it unless you are stating facts. Because I founded a women's organisation, I will comment on what I have directly experienced or actual statistics.

- **Dress as if everyone is looking at you, because they are!** Male or female, keep your outfit simple and professional. This is when you need to look at every aspect of what you have on. If you have to go on a stage, remember people are looking up, so give the short skirt a miss. Look your best, but don't let it distract from what you are saying.

And as an added bonus, here is my checklist I use for every presentation with some added points and notes:

- Slides have been checked by a fresh set of eyes.

- Presentation has been sent to the organiser and is also on my laptop, and on an extra USB in my bag.

- My laptop is fully charged and the charger is in my bag.

- I have confirmed with the organiser the layout of the room and what time I can access the room before the presentation.

- A lapel mic has been requested. (This is much easier than a handheld mic.)

- I have confirmed what the number of attendees will be and have asked for a list. (Getting a list means you can check out on LinkedIn who will be there – always a good idea.)

- I have requested that water be available, and tissues. (Although I always bring my own just in case.)

- If needed, I have requested a whiteboard in advance, and have packed markers. (Bringing your own markers ensures you have good ones.)

- I have prepared handouts as needed. (Not all presentations require handouts. However, if your presentation does, make sure your handouts have been checked. I prefer to tell attendees that I will email them a handout after the presentation. If the organiser cannot give you emails, bring hard copies and make these available after the presentation.)

- Thank-you note or email has been sent to the organiser after the event.

Focus on why you are there and the message that you want to get across.

Whether you are presenting to a group of women or a group of men shouldn't affect your approach. Instead, focus on the impression you want the audience to have of you as an individual. Don't bring sex into public, bring you.

CHAPTER SIX

No Sex as the New Manager

In this chapter, I cover issues you may encounter as a first-time manager, or an experienced manager going into a new position.

As I covered in the previous chapter, from the moment you step into any new role, it is not about your sex; it is about your individual performance and what you can do to increase your chances of success. The company has hired you for a reason, and that reason is to do a good job. This is even more important if you have been hired to a management position.

The word 'manager' having 'man' in it does not mean manager is a gender-specific role. Sex does not define who is good at being a manager and who is not. The behaviours and leadership qualities you exhibit as an individual will define your success as a manager, not your gender.

Whether you're a first-timer or experienced manager, the first months in any new role will set the scene for how you are perceived by others. Therefore, it is very important to start off on the right foot.

If we go back to the schoolyard analogy in chapter 4, in this position you are the new teacher. From day one, you will have students/employees, the principal/boss and the other teachers/stakeholders checking you out until you prove yourself.

You will need to manage bullies, teacher's pets, geeks, gurus and a whole range of personalities that you didn't even know existed. You will be expected to lead through change, motivate during downturns, fix systems, bring in business, manage conflicts and be a leader all at the same time. Leadership is challenging even without bringing sex into the equation.

Are you an imposter or is it in your head?

The minute you step into the office (schoolyard), you may start to experience self-doubt and question whether this job is bigger than you thought. All the chatter in your head is based on information that you have heard and read in the past. You might, for example, remember an article on imposter syndrome and say to yourself, 'Maybe this is me? Am I a fraud?'

I have heard many people talk about imposter syndrome as if it is something new; however, it is really just another name for what was more traditionally known as self-doubt. In fact, even the term 'impostor syndrome' is not new and was first identified by psychologists in 1978. Why is it still being identified as an issue as if it is a new discovery?

Imposter syndrome is the feeling you get when you think something you have been given – such as a new role or project – is not warranted and that you are a fraud and not deserving. You don't accept your achievements and fear others will find out that you are not as capable as they originally thought you were.

I've noticed women are especially good at telling themselves that they are an imposter. Why don't I hear the guys say it?

REFLECTION

Have you experienced feelings of being an 'imposter' about to be exposed? What do you think might be behind these feelings?

When I started my executive search firm, I was recruiting for a general manager position and had never held a general manager role myself. So did that make me an imposter?

I didn't see myself as an imposter because I didn't represent myself to the client as someone with general manager experience. The client knew my background and hired me because of my skills in finding talented candidates and bringing them to the table.

I didn't need years in the role I was hiring for; I only needed to obtain enough knowledge about the role to be able to seek out appropriate candidates, conduct the interviews and advise my client on who I believed was the strongest contender. I was more than capable of doing the assignment. I just needed to gather the required information. Not once did I feel I was an imposter, because I represented myself accurately to the client.

If you don't overstate your experience in your interview, you will never be an imposter.

You have been hired for the management position because of your experience and the skills you displayed in the interview. If it turns out when you start the role that some of the required responsibilities are beyond what was discussed in the interview process, have the conversation with your boss and be open about the skills and experience you do and don't have. Stress that you are excited to learn new skills. This will help you get off on the right foot and will avoid any misunderstandings.

Executives I have spoken to in the past all say that out of ten 'boxes' required for a role, they hire the person who ticks six. They do not want someone who ticks all the boxes and gets bored in the position after three months. Your new boss is not expecting you to tick every box.

Your boss wants someone who will grow into the role and be there for the next three years. So it is not necessary to overstate what you have done or pretend you have everything covered when you don't, because most companies want someone who will grow into the position. If you still have 'imposter' feelings – or what I prefer to simply call self-doubt – read on.

Self-doubt as a manager

Some things you will be good at and others you won't. A good manager is someone who can identify their weaknesses and bring in the right people to complement their skills.

In my businesses I knew every function, but I wasn't great at everything – and nor did I want to do everything. As a manager, you should know your strengths and weaknesses and understand that having self-doubt is part of your growth.

No matter your gender, you should never feel that you need to be smarter than the members of your team in everything. You are there to lead, give direction and inspire. If you don't know an answer, you will be expected to find the solution. Don't be the manager who thinks they know it all and then makes mistakes because of their arrogance. Be a T10P and ask questions and admit to the things you don't know so you can find the answers.

My first boss said to me, 'Always hire people who are smarter than you. They will make you and the area you are managing look good'.

The T10Ps at every level in their career have doubts, and that is one of the reasons they are great leaders.

They question if they should go ahead with a new project and wonder if it will be successful. The mere fact that they do question themselves means they are analysing the situation. A T10P is confident enough to see their own weakness and bring in the appropriate resources to overcome them.

Having self-doubt and questioning your capabilities to get a clearer picture of where you need help is a good trait. This is a sign of a good leader.

How to handle self-doubt

Self-doubt never goes away; you will experience it at every stage of your career. You just learn to handle it better as you build your confidence.

I recommend looking at self-doubt differently; that is, not as something to hide, as if you have done something wrong and will be caught out, but as an opportunity for growth. Experiencing self-doubt is your chance to ascertain whether you need more training in a particular area, or if the experience you have is enough and you're underestimating yourself.

I never recommend masking self-doubt, or trying to 'fake it till you make it'. If your self-doubt is pointing to skills that you need to develop, take this on board and do something about it.

Don't risk having something fall through the cracks that could jeopardise your job or the company.

I have self-doubt all the time, but I am still confident that I can do whatever I set my mind to do. If I realise that I am not up to the task, I will find someone who can help. It's not a failure – it's a realisation.

REFLECTION

So how is your self-doubt? And who do you think has more self-doubt? Men or women? I definitely have experienced women having more self-doubt at work. Is it a gender thing? Or have men just learnt to mask it better?

From what I have seen, men seem to be better at hiding feelings of self-doubt. This could be from being told at an early age not to show emotion. In my experience, however, I have also noticed that men have more mentors during their career journey, providing them support. This could also help to squash self-doubt.

Maybe men are just better at masking their self-doubt because they are so often told to show no fear. Mentors often tell them, 'Get the role and worry about it later'.

Women, on the other hand, can let self-doubt stop them from progressing and will often think they have less experience than they actually have. As a result, their self-doubt may prevent them going forward or taking a chance on a new role. They tend to underplay their experience and are often pushed to apply for opportunities (as I discuss further in chapter 8). They don't have the same support systems as the men, to bounce their feelings of self-doubt off of, so they back out and retreat. If they do take the new role, all the feelings of self-doubt about not being capable continue into the role.

How many times have you noticed a gender difference when it came to people you work with showing self-doubt? Do people in your team now immediately say no to something new? Is it just their self-doubt kicking in? And what about yourself? Do you tend to back off from the unknown because of your own self-doubt?

Self-doubt becomes an issue for your progress when you let it linger for too long and don't address it.

If you're letting self-doubt talk you out of good opportunities, or masking it or sweeping it under the rug, you need to address it. If you don't, issues could arise later.

When you communicate accurately your experience level and capabilities with your new boss, you may find that you have the level of experience needed or you need to upskill; either way, you know where you stand and so does your boss.

I handle my own self-doubt by saying, 'So what if I don't have *xyz*? What I don't know, I will learn'.

I don't wait for someone else to convince me that I can do something. I don't apologise for what I don't know. I am honest with myself about my capabilities and decide whether the required skill is something I can learn or something I should outsource.

Once you have identified that you are having self-doubt, deal with these feelings through action – for example, work out a plan to upskill on what you don't have. There has been a first time for everything you have ever done in your life, so why should this be any different?

REFLECTION

How aware are you of your own weaknesses and gaps?

When I first went into executive search, a friend suggested that I do a Myers-Briggs Type Indicator test as a way of seeing what my strengths and weaknesses were.

While the science behind this test has been questioned, I have always found the process worthwhile. When the results came back in this case, they showed I was a strong opener. This meant opening conversations with clients came easily to me.

The test also showed, however, that I was a weak closer. This meant closing the deal with a client was a weakness. I knew that if I wanted to grow my business, I needed to learn to be a good closer.

I didn't make excuses and say the test was not right or question the validity of it. I looked at what it showed very closely and what I could do to change this result. What skills would I need to improve to become a good closer?

I worked hard to improve my closing skills and found three things needed to happen: I needed to listen to the client more, ask good questions, and ask for the business at the end of the meeting.

I took the test again 12 months later and this time I came out as a stronger closer than I was an opener.

If I hadn't embraced my weakness and improved my closing skills, I would not have succeeded in my business.

Don't see what you can't do as a weakness – see it as something you haven't learnt yet, but will.

Kick arrogance out the door

Arrogance could be seen as the opposite of self-doubt, but is usually a manager's way of diverting attention away from a weakness they have. An arrogant manager would never consider themselves to be an imposter; instead, they are blinded by their own self-importance. They don't ask the necessary questions because they think everything they do is perfect. They very rarely ask for help and never admit to mistakes. They do not like critique and will accuse others who give constructive feedback as being negative people. As a new manager, don't go into your new role thinking you know everything; it's never a good look to be seen as arrogant.

Arrogance is not gender-specific

If you think only men can be arrogant, think again. Being self-obsessed is not a gender-specific trait. Unfortunately, I have met a lot of arrogant people over the years of both genders, and what makes them arrogant is over-confidence that isn't justified.

A client once said to me about one of his direct reports, 'He is better than he looks, but not as good as he thinks'.

That to me was the best description for most arrogant people – male and female. Probably somewhere in their upbringing they were told how great they were all the time and never held to account.

While researching for this book, I came across the Dunning–Kruger effect, which basically outlines how people with low ability at a task often think they are smarter or more competent than they really are. What a surprise! After 25-plus years dealing with executives, I could have saved them a lot of research! Companies are full of people suffering from the Dunning–Kruger effect. (Interestingly, the same effect outlines how, as people increase their abilities, they often initially underestimate how competent they are.)

One of the most common words I have heard candidates use to describe their boss is 'arrogant'. Arrogant managers were often cited as a reason for excellent candidates deciding to resign from their positions. If you are a manager, are you losing people in your team because they misunderstand you?

Is your confidence being viewed as arrogance?

Making an impression in your first 12 months

The first 12 months of any job can be hard. You will need to put in extra time and effort to come up to speed and make an impression.

As mentioned in chapter 4, just as any new employee should do, make sure you ask your boss what they expect of you as a new manager. You are the boss for your team, and you have a boss as well, so you need to communicate with your new boss just like your team should communicate with you.

When the excitement of getting the new management role has passed, you will ask yourself one or several of the following questions, sometime between your first day and up to 12 months, and often depending on your gender and your age. Along with listing these common questions, I've also included how to respond to them.

If you are a woman:

■ *Are the guys in the team going to resent me because they think I got this job because of a quota?*

Some people may think this way in organisations that are quota-focused. I say – their problem, not yours. Organisations don't put people in roles they think will fail. You are there because of your capabilities and because the company has faith in you, so block out the negatives and focus on what you will bring to the role.

■ *Are the women going to resent me because I am a woman and they aren't used to working for a female?*

I've had women say to me in interviews that they do not want to work for a female manager because of a bad experience. When I delved deeper, they had also had bad experiences with at least one male boss, so I would ask, 'Does that mean you won't work for a man as well?' This attitude is definitely there, but I believe it is in the minority. Just put your focus on good management skills to win your staff over.

◈ *Do I need to change my style and be more direct like the guys?*

Part of no sex at work is being you, not someone else – that is, taking you to work and applying the business skills needed to be a good manager. Take your personality and capabilities and blend these with what a businessperson needs to do in order to be successful. Don't be someone else – you do you.

If you are a man:

◈ *Are the women in the team going to resent me because they feel a woman should have been appointed?*

If the company does not have a good diversity policy in place along with a fair recruitment process, it is highly likely that women in your team will be upset. It will be up to you as the new manager to put in place equality measures and to change the culture, so gender is not an issue for the next appointment. Show your team that you believe in no sex at work.

◈ *Should I behave differently around female staff versus the male staff?*

The short answer is no. For more detail, check out the next chapter.

If you are young:

◈ *I am younger than most of the people on the team and don't have the same experience as some of the other team members. What will the older ones think? How do I get credibility?*

Look at what you know and what you don't know. Put steps in place to upskill as needed and gain credibility with your team by being upfront and learning what you don't know. Don't think about your age; think about what you need to do as a good manager. Age is only a number. (For more on how I dealt with this issue, see the Reflection on the next page.)

For men and women:

■ *If I fail, how is it going to look?*

You are going to fail at a lot of things. My view is if you don't fail occasionally, you aren't doing enough. It is how you fail that is important. Do you take defeat graciously or do you blame others? Failure only looks bad if you behave in a way that is seen as unprofessional.

■ *I need to manage my friends in the team. Will they treat me differently and how do I treat them?*

Your friends will likely treat you differently, because now you are their boss. In the work environment, you need to treat them in the same way as all your other staff. Set parameters and don't let them take liberties because you are friends. The rest of your team will notice any preferential treatment and not like it – and it will damage your brand as a fair manager. In addition, do not discuss work issues that don't concern them with your friends.

This is only a sample of the questions you may ask yourself, but they are the ones that I have heard continually over the years.

Who is on the bus?

In my 25-plus years of interviewing the most successful managers in the financial services industry, I have always asked them the following interview question: 'When you take on a new role, what is the first thing you do?' Consistently, the top performers reply along the lines of, 'I get to know the staff on a human level and find out *who is on the bus*'.

They explain that they take staff for a coffee and break down any barriers to find out about them as individuals – what makes them tick, if they are happy, how they feel about the job and the company, and if they have a positive or negative attitude.

Finding out 'who is on the bus' is something I first heard from my boss in the early eighties. Basically, if you are on the bus, you are a team player with a good attitude, and you're supportive of the company's strategy going forward.

As a new manager, understanding your team is vital for success. This is as essential for the first-time manager as it is for a seasoned manager going into a new role. If someone in the new team is not on the bus, you need to sort it out quickly – either through providing coaching to fix the situation, or letting them off at the next stop.

REFLECTION

Are you letting your self-doubt stand in the way of getting to the heart of matters with your staff?

When I got my first management position at a young age, I had so many doubts, but my upbringing gave me the confidence to just go for it. Gender wasn't causing me to doubt myself - it was my age and lack of experience that scared me.

When applying for the role, I thought I wouldn't have chance in a million years because of how many people in the team had more experience than me. I thought it would be good experience to put my hand up anyway and let management know I was interested in advancement. To my surprise, I got the role.

Another guy in particular in the team had applied and was not happy that I got the role and he didn't. He was about 40 at the time and very experienced.

He did everything possible to make my life miserable in my first few weeks as the new manager. I thought, *This has got to stop and I need to confront him*.

I asked him into my office and said, 'I know you are upset that I'm in this role and you feel you should be. You have so much more experience than me, but don't get mad at me for getting the role. Get mad at yourself for not getting the role. My guess is your attitude had something to do with it'.

He looked at me and asked me what I meant. I said to him that he probably went into the process thinking he had it in the bag and that likely came across as complacency or arrogance. When they interviewed me, on the other hand, they saw passion and growth.

I said to him that I had skills and capabilities when it came to relationship-building and he had technical skills – so we could help each other. Once he realised I was not the enemy, we worked well together, and both learnt from each other.

If you remember the schoolyard analogy from chapter 4, this person was a combination of the school bully and one of the geeks. Once you confront a bully, they often will back down and sometimes they will work with you.

If he hadn't been prepared to work with me, as a new manager, I would have had to make a call and let the bully go. If I didn't, it would have sent a message to the rest of my team that I was willing to accept bad behaviour. Being young and female didn't mean I couldn't stand up for myself.

If you find yourself in a similar situation, try to remember this story and know there are no limitations in standing up for yourself.

Your message builds your brand

Remember how children watch every move their parents make? The same is the case for your staff – they are watching your every move, particularly when you first begin to manage the team. Your staff are guided by you and influenced by your behaviour – both verbal and non-verbal.

If you cut corners, your staff will cut corners; if you come in late, they will come in late; if you tell a client off, they will treat clients the same way.

Don't treat genders differently. If you are a male boss, don't treat the boys in your team differently to the girls. Treat everyone equally.

One of the biggest mistakes new managers make is not paying attention to building and applying soft skills, especially when they start. Soft skills such as communication, teamwork and conflict resolution are what will set you apart from the crowd.

And keep in mind the common courtesies from chapter 4 because they apply for new managers as well. To re-cap: say hello to your staff in the morning. Keep positive and be the motivator because your staff will look to you for inspiration. Don't levelise people and treat everyone with equal respect. This will build your brand not only with your team, but also with other staff in your organisation.

Remember, as a manager your reputation with upper management and others across the organisation depends on your team's behaviour. If your team members consistently display bad habits or your team has high turnover, this will reflect poorly on you.

REFLECTION

What do you think your reputation with upper management and across the business is?

I was once recruiting for an executive manager role for one of my best clients. Let's call him Dave. Dave always exhibited T10P qualities and had a great reputation in the industry.

He was very good at leading and hired people smarter than him because he knew how to address his weaknesses. He was great at the common courtesies and treated everyone with respect, which built his brand not only in his area, but also across the company.

When the position (reporting to Dave) was posted on the internal job board, it received the biggest response from candidates outside the division of any position that I had ever seen. It also received the highest number of women applying internally, so I didn't need to tap anyone on the shoulder.

The candidates who applied said they had heard Dave was a great manager and they wanted to work for him. Dave's reputation as a good leader had gone beyond his own area and filtered through to other departments in the organisation.

His strong leadership traits had not gone unnoticed and that is why his career went from strength to strength.

What do you think you could change right now, to start building a reputation within your organisation similar to Dave's?

Hold on to your best people

A new manager being brought into a team can cause disruption among team members. Often, team members have a great relationship with the previous manager and feel unsure about their future in the organisation and whether they want to stay on board.

Some people can't imagine working for anyone else, so you need to make them feel secure and let them know that you are there for the right reasons. You need to be someone they want to work for. Remember – high achievers have options, and they want to work for people they admire. How you treat people will make the difference between you being a T10P and you being one of the arrogant managers who talk big, with few results.

When I was a headhunter and heard changes had occurred in a team, I would find out who the high performers in that team were and approach them for the opportunities I had on my books. Headhunters always know which companies are going through change, so make sure you are communicating with your new team and making a good impression – so the best workers aren't enticed to leave.

REFLECTION

How can you work to communicate with your new team and ensure how you act matches what you say?

In my role as an executive search consultant, I was privy to many situations. In one case, a company had new managers coming into the business. The current team was high-performing and passionate about the business. The company was doing really well and additional managers were hired to take the company to its next level of success.

The team accepted the changes and were initially excited. The problems started when the new managers started to levelise. They treated existing staff in dismissive ways and didn't listen to their ideas or acknowledge their expertise. They often didn't return their calls or emails and didn't spend time getting to know the team or the existing business.

The new managers' behaviours were not consistent with what was coming out of their mouths. They would talk about leadership, but didn't know how to lead. They spoke about productivity, but were not productive. They didn't practise what they preached and sent inconsistent messages.

Staff started leaving for new opportunities and business was walking out the door. All the good work of building a high-performing business was imploding because the new managers were not following new manager guidelines.

Senior management didn't figure out what was happening until it was too late because the new managers would blame everyone else.

How many times have you seen this? How can you do things differently?

In the example in the preceding Reflection, the new team was equal in gender, so sex had nothing to do with their behaviours. It had to do with how they were taught from their early upbringing and school days, and into the work environment. They displayed all the traits of the schoolyard bullies, and the mean girls and the mean boys. When they left school and moved into the work environment, they probably learnt from other schoolyard friends with bad habits. Make sure your role models are T10Ps.

Final steps to success as a new manager

As some final tips, here are some simple guidelines to cover the basics of your first month as a new manager:

- **Let your team know how you want to communicate:** Do you want to communicate via email or a meeting once a week? Set timelines for everything so they know when things are due. Be consistent in your message. Treat everyone equally.

- **Outline your expectations when returning calls, emails and texts:** Don't underestimate this rule of engagement, because not following best practice will set a precedent for your team that anything is acceptable – and one person's view of what is acceptable may be different from others'.

- **Ensure that each of your team members has a clear position description and measurable outcomes:** The last thing you want is for your staff to say they don't know what they need to do. Your manager could hear this and this will be a direct reflection on you, not your staff. If you have joined a company that does not have good position descriptions, take the time to revise and improve the standard.

- **Organise an initial meeting with your staff and a follow-up:** Find out who is on the bus and get to know your staff. Make sure to schedule a follow-up meeting because you want to keep a handle on how they are going and if any issues have arisen. I would recommend doing the follow-up at the two-month mark.

- **Listen to the feedback from current staff:** Learn what is working and what isn't. One of the biggest mistakes new managers make is not getting to know the business they are going into and trying to make change too quickly. Listen to the staff who are on the bus because they may have something important to contribute.

- **Accept mistakes will happen and ensure they don't happen again:** Set high standards and encourage staff to provide critiques – and ensure any critique and feedback is accepted and welcomed.

- **Lead by example:** Remember the saying, 'Practise what you preach'? It is very important that your team sees you implementing what is coming out of your mouth and what you tell them they need to do.

Being a good manager in a new job has lots of layers involved. I have covered the basics here that should help you get on the right track. Remember – you need to have the technical skills and capabilities to do the job, but the company doesn't expect you to tick every box. Embrace your self-doubt and recognise that it is all part of the journey.

CHAPTER SEVEN

No Sex Talk

As a manager, it may seem harder to know what to say these days compared to years ago when people had no filters and said what they liked. But this is a good thing! It is good to see that the world is changing and unacceptable language is being called out; however, more work is still to be done. With different generations working together, some confusion still exists about what is acceptable and what isn't.

If we want to keep sex out of the workforce, with a no gender focus and true equality, we need to pay close attention to what we are saying and the messages our words send – both verbally and via written communication.

REFLECTION

What experiences have you had when the words chosen, and the message behind them, could have been better?

In one of my first roles in banking, I reported to a manager who was around 20 years my senior. He was English and was used to addressing women – and especially the younger women – as 'love'.

The first time he said, 'Love, would you do *xyz* for me, please', I was taken by surprise, because no-one had ever called me 'love' before. I thought, *No way is this guy going to call me 'love'*. And I started thinking about how I was going to get him to stop.

I didn't want to make a big fuss and go to HR to complain, and instead remembered what my grandmother used to say about catching more bees with honey.

The next time he addressed me as 'love', I replied, 'I don't have a problem with you calling me "love", as long as you don't have a problem with me replying, "Okay, sweetie".' He paused and I could tell he was thinking, and then he said, 'Point taken'.

I addressed the issue in a light-hearted way to make the point without harming our working relationship, and in this case it worked perfectly. He also stopped calling the other girls 'love', so I saw it as a win for all of us.

If someone is saying something you are uncomfortable with, try to resolve it then and there. If it doesn't get resolved, escalate it immediately.

How are you addressing your staff and colleagues?

Language in the work environment has the ability to set the tone of what is acceptable in that organisation. If managers are calling their staff 'sweetie', 'honey', 'babe' or 'doll' (these are real examples I have recently heard), this will not reflect well on the organisation. Staff will, at best, be offended or, at worst, think the behaviour is acceptable and appropriate.

It is not just men who use pet names for their colleagues; women are also guilty of this. Take a moment to think about whether you are calling anyone at work by anything other than their given name, and how this could be perceived.

REFLECTION

Do you or your staff use pet names or nicknames in the workplace? What sort of effect do you think this has?

Connie Mckeage (CEO of OneVue, 2020 Women in Finance CEO of the Year and FEW advisory board member) is someone I admire for her direct approach. Connie is passionate about equality for everyone. She told me the following story about a situation she experienced at OneVue:

A few years ago, we were having a OneVue offsite for the management team. In order to free the team to concentrate on the agenda and focus on the issues, I hired an external facilitator to manage the process. I had met with the facilitator a few times to agree on the agenda and order of events but that was the limit of the interaction before the offsite. To my knowledge, everyone had heard of the facilitator but no-one knew him.

The day of the offsite arrived and one of my team members, 'Harry' (not his real name), asked if it was okay if he could arrive a bit late because he had to drop his kids off at school. I said, 'Of course, get there when you get there'.

So, the day started without Harry and, as was expected, everyone introduced themselves and engaged with the facilitator. The mood was positive and everyone felt that they had equal say and that all opinions were being valued equally.

About an hour into the session Harry entered the room through a side door. At this stage, we had divided into groups and were working through various scenarios and the facilitator was moving from one group to another. However, when the facilitator saw Harry enter the room he stopped what he was doing and went towards him, saying, 'Killer! Welcome – so good to have you here'.

I always tell this story during our OneVue staff inductions to explain what happened in that moment. The use of a nickname was a blatant display of the familiarity between Harry and the facilitator. It broke the sense of equality in the room. When I later asked what happened in that moment for everyone, people told me that not only was there a sense of favouritism and familiarity, but the interaction also rightly or wrongly led to certain individuals feeling they no longer had an equal voice, or that information would be shared informally to one person that was not readily available to the rest.

That's when I decided that, in order to genuinely promote inclusion, I had to eliminate certain behaviours that led to people feeling excluded - and using nicknames was one of these. When I came back into the office on the following day and announced that everyone was to use their colleagues' proper names, the silence at first was deafening - and then employee after employee came in to thank me for taking a stand. The first person that came into my office was a man who said, 'I have hated my nickname all my life. It's bad enough my friends call me that, but I also had to put up with it at work'.

Out of all the things I have implemented to support inclusion, that one small act has had the broadest and deepest impact. It is about not only gender diversity, but also inclusion.

We can establish diversity committees and say we support diversity but unless we are willing to stand up for the things that occur day to day in our organisations, we will only be paying lip-service to real change.

Connie's example highlights just one of many situations where people call others pet names. In this example, the facilitator calling Harry 'Killer' was very 'blokey', which could also leave the women in the team feeling as if it were a boys' club.

Are you the recipient of a nickname yourself and does it bother you? Or do you use nicknames or allow your staff to? Then speak up and tell people that you would like to be called your preferred name. Don't put up with a nickname or someone calling you 'sweetie' or 'love' or anything else that is not your name. And don't put up with this behaviour from your staff either.

If you are a manager, be a leader like Connie and set new rules of engagement for your team on what they call each other.

Connie is right: people calling others by nicknames is likely to make the other people in the room feel uncomfortable. They will see a familiarity and will feel left out. The goal is to make everyone feel equal. In addition, some of those nicknames could be sexist or discriminatory (such as calling someone 'big guy', not knowing that they are sensitive about their weight).

If you want to take one easy step for your organisation on the path towards no sex at work and true equality, put in place a rule of engagement for nicknames immediately, as Connie did. I will even write it for you:

> *To ensure we are building a culture for true equality and inclusion, as of [date] all staff are required to call each other by their preferred given names. No nicknames or generic terms are to be used when addressing someone in the workplace. This is one easy step that will help all staff feel they are included equally in conversations and at meetings as part of a united team.*

What if you called work colleagues by the name they introduced themselves with when you first met them? How would this change your culture?

Flirting at work

Many people meet their partners at work, especially in large organisations. What do you, as a single person in a management position, do if you are interested in someone in your organisation?

I am going to be very blunt here: do nothing and move on!

Flirting with your staff or anyone in your organisation is a bad idea. If the relationship breaks down or the attention is not reciprocated, things may not end well. You could even lose your job if things go awry.

If you let yourself be drawn into sex talk at work, words you are using that you think are innocent and playful could be making others feel uncomfortable. Here are some examples:

- 'You look hot in that outfit!'
- 'Are you dating anyone?'
- 'What does your girlfriend think of you having a female boss?'
- 'What does your boyfriend think of you working late hours?'
- 'Have you ever considered dating someone older?'
- 'Would you like to discuss that project over drinks?'

Think about what you are saying and if it is worth losing a career you have worked hard to get. Depending on the situation, the statements in the preceding list could be taken as sexual harassment. When in doubt if something is appropriate or not, ask for a confidential discussion with your human resources representative.

When I was in my early twenties, we didn't have social media and if the relationship didn't work, people could easily move on without many people knowing. This lack of information flow unfortunately protected unwanted perpetrators as well.

Today, gossip can follow you around for the rest of your career. What some see as innocent fun, others may find intimidating. If you always remember that work is work and social activity happens outside of work, it will be easier to keep work professional. Don't be one of the ones who learns the lesson the hard way by losing their job.

Having a reputation for office flirting can also hurt your chances of being hired at different organisations. When I reference checked candidates, if they had a reputation for inappropriate behaviour, the referee might say something like, 'They had a way with the girls and that became an issue'.

Those candidates never went forward because I felt they would be a risk to the company. The candidate never knew why they really didn't progress because references are confidential.

Most people don't know how to handle unwanted advances and are not confident to speak up in the moment. Making someone uncomfortable at work is never okay, no matter your position or intentions.

Bringing sex into the work environment is so unproductive.

If companies could encourage their staff to talk about these issues openly and agree on what is acceptable behaviour and language, it would go a long way to getting sex out of work.

When social and work communication collide

Christmas parties, functions and conferences have killed many a career. I am always amazed that management do not make it clear that these functions are not opportunities to drink until everyone is saying any stupid thing that comes out of their mouth. Often, the leadership team is right in there with the rest of the group with big regrets the next day. While these events are tagged as 'social' functions, they are still work functions. This is something that should be made clear to everyone attending.

These guidelines should have been available and discussed with staff prior to any event.

This type of story is very common and I have heard and seen similar versions many times over the years. The results are also similar – someone resigns, or someone is fired and careers are damaged.

Does your company have social guidelines in place? Do you discuss these with staff before events and ensure they are followed?

When I attended industry conferences or work events with my staff, I had two rules:

1. Keep one full drink in front of you so people don't pester you to drink. (And I didn't mean keep drinking and filling up that drink.)

2. At cocktail events, do the rounds to say hello to clients and leave by 9.00 pm because after that they won't remember you.

My view was we were at these events to work – to make connections with our clients and have a clear mind when we spoke so we could keep track of our purpose. Alcohol loosens the tongue and people often say things they regret.

I didn't apologise for my strict guidelines around work functions and no-one complained. I explained my reasons and they understood. We all saw people who didn't have similar rules in place make complete idiots of themselves, saying inappropriate things to others and putting their companies at risk of litigation.

In today's environment, having strict policies to prevent issues with sex talk makes good business sense.

As I write this, a scandal has just erupted that has cost someone (let's call him 'Alvin') their career. I don't know all the facts – just that media reports have outlined photos and text messages were involved. Many people I spoke to were surprised and had no knowledge of this kind of behaviour from Alvin. I, too, was shocked, because that had not been my experience either.

I don't know if Alvin is guilty of what was said or not. The accusers did not come forward publicly and the journalist grabbed the story and was ruthless in their pursuit, so it's hard to know if what was reported was proven.

In the case of corporate gossip, however, mud sticks whether you are innocent or guilty. Once a rumour starts, it is hard to stop.

If we go back to Ted from the previous Reflection, he was a senior person similar to Alvin. If, as a manager, you think that it is okay to put the moves on your staff and your secret will be safe, think again. Remember Bill Clinton? If the most powerful man in the world can't keep a relationship a secret, what chance have you got?

Alvin and Ted both made poor judgement calls. Both were single and thought it was okay. But if someone is made to feel uncomfortable, then it is not okay, under any circumstance.

If it were me and I were in a corporate role again, I would not date anyone in my organisation. If you work for a large organisation, other divisions can be like separate companies so exceptions may exist.

However, the Teds and Alvins of the world, along with anyone in a senior role, should know that dating staff is not a good idea. Even taking the chance of asking someone out who is not interested could be seen as flirting or harassment. That person could then say the reason they are not getting promoted is because they knocked you back for a date.

Despite both these examples being men, it isn't only men in power positions making a move on younger staff. I've heard examples of senior women making younger men feel uncomfortable.

People in positions of power must realise they have certain responsibilities of care, no matter their gender.

What if you meet someone you really like?

In some cases people have met their partner at work. They usually are at the same level or, if one is more senior, someone decides to move companies or divisions. Starting a relationship at work is a big risk and a decision to take seriously. I know if you're young and single you will likely question the reality of keeping relationships out of the work environment; however, really think it through.

If you still decide that you are going to date someone at work (even though I told you not to!), keep the following in mind:

- Be very certain that the person you are asking out is interested. If you ask them out and they say no, do not ask again and be polite in your response to the rejection.

- If you are in a romantic relationship with someone at work, do not send anything via text or email that you would not want to see on the front page of a newspaper.

- If the person you are dating is in your department, someone needs to transfer. Your staff will know and if your partner gets a promotion – even a deserved one – it will be seen as favouritism no matter what. Every time you go out to lunch together people will talk.

- Let your HR area know that you are dating someone in the business and see if you need to follow any specific protocols. In fact, you should check your HR policies before you even ask someone out, because some companies have a no-dating policy for employees.

Outdated sex talk

It's not just inappropriate sex talk that needs to go; what about the things we constantly hear that separate genders and stop the work environment from being totally equal?

Numerous statements and words are used every day that we accept – statements that give an incorrect impression of a gender or group and need to be eliminated from the work environment, so we have no sex at work. When we hear them, we need to call it out and educate, so sex talk is no longer an issue.

Let's look at some of the most common things both men and women say that promote damaging gender stereotypes – and how to deal with them.

Women are emotional and will cry if you confront them

This is not a gender issue – it is a resilience issue. How do you handle pressure, and what happens if you fail? I have never cried at work and I have been confronted with lots of negative situations that could have pushed me over. I have learnt to take a breath and know that whatever happens, it is not the end of the world. I am sure, however, that I have made several men cry in my past!

Women are not fragile and this perception is so damaging. Leaders need to be strong to handle the ups and downs of business; however, excluding women as not strong enough would be very discrim-inatory. When looking at who to appoint for a role that needed someone to tackle change in the organisation, for example, men and women should be considered equally.

Women don't know how to play the game or network like the men

In any new job, you need to network and find out who the stakeholders are. I was lucky to have the right mentors who taught me the importance of networking, so I could put this into practice from day one in my career. Men aren't better networkers simply because they are men; instead, they may seem to be because they had a network early in their careers who taught them the ropes. All genders are equally capable of networking, and you shouldn't let your gender get in the way of such an essential strategy for career progression.

Women are perfectionists and won't delegate

Women are not born to be perfectionists. They may become perfectionists because they are so worried that they will make a mistake and jeopardise their job. This often means they are not prepared to risk their work being incorrect and have it reflect poorly on them. This is compounded by women being the minority in management roles and so feeling more judged by any mistake. Men have no problem delegating, because somewhere down the line one of their mentors told them to make sure they are passing work to their staff so they can focus on more important items. Again, this highlights the importance of mentors! (See the section 'No means no', later in this chapter, for more on delegating.)

She is in a bad mood today; must be that time of month

This is usually women speaking about other women, which is unfortunate. I have personally heard this many times over the years and it is very annoying. Women leaders who are not coming across as happy and conversational can often be accused as being cold or mad about something – or hormonal. Men will be seen as serious and focused. Keep sex out of any perceptions and look instead at the behaviour – and how that might be improved.

She won't relocate; she has a family

This is a presumption by both genders that will limit getting the best candidate for the job. The family unit is very different these days and relocation opportunities are not gender-specific.

No means no

There is one word at work that clearly has a gender difference in its usage, and that is the word 'no'.

Women often tell me they have a hard time saying no at work and take on additional tasks others really should be doing. Men, on the other hand, don't seem to have that problem. Men tend to have mentors in their corner who have told them to only take on things that will help them personally, and to delegate the rest. Men don't see saying no as damaging to their brand. They have been taught how to say no and what to say yes to.

During our mentoring group sessions at FEW, learning how to say no is the most asked-about topic. The members often felt they were being taken advantage of, and that people thought they were an easy target. They also saw the guys saying no all the time and no-one holding it against them. When I asked why they didn't say no, some common answers were as follows:

- They feared being seen as unhelpful or a b***h.

- It seemed okay to say yes at first, but then they found out the thing they had said yes to was taking too much time.

- They were 'people pleasers' and found it hard to knock anyone back.

▪ They didn't know the correct way to say it, so they said yes and then regretted it.

The first thing they want to know is, 'How do I say no in a way that isn't seen as mean and doesn't damage my brand?'

If you have similar questions, I'll say the same thing to you as I tell them: take gender out of your head in that moment. Are you feeling this way because you have seen other women say no and there was a backlash? Or are you letting your own fear of what may or may not happen get in your way of saying no?

Before you respond to a request, take a step back to think about what you are potentially saying yes or no to. How you respond is not based on a gender trait; it is a business skill that is learnt and is based on analysing what is important and what isn't.

Here are some suggestions to help with your analysis before you respond:

▪ **Context is important:** Who is asking you – your boss or a colleague? In the case of your boss, if you have a full to-do list, clarify the importance of the task. Just because your boss is asking, it doesn't mean you should automatically say yes – especially if doing so is at the cost of another important task. Find out by saying something like, 'Yes, I can do that, but it will mean that I will need to stop x or y'. This often reveals how important the new request really is and then your boss can give you permission to put another task on your list on hold.

▪ **Ask for more time:** If you feel blindsided and are inclined to say yes by default, then try saying, 'I can't give you an answer right now as I will need to look at my priorities and will let you know by the end of the day' (or whatever timeline works with the request). That will give you crucial time to analyse pros and cons.

- **Ask for more information:** If asked to deliver something you don't believe you could deliver, seek more information to understand the request. If you do say yes, also specify a realistic completion time – because if you say yes and don't deliver or take longer to deliver than expected, it will come back on you and will damage your brand.

- **Be courteous:** Don't respond with a blunt no but rather something like, 'Thanks for asking me; however, I don't feel I would be able to put in the time this project deserves and I wouldn't want to let you down, so for now I will decline'.

- **Highlight your existing priorities:** If a co-worker is asking you to do something that will interfere with getting your job done, highlight this for them. Say something like, 'I would really love to help you, but I have other priorities that need to be done by *xyz*. If I didn't have these priorities, I would be more than happy to help'. Or, 'Thank you for asking me, it sounds like a great project. However, given all my other priorities, I don't feel I could dedicate the time to it that it deserves'.

The key to saying no professionally is to be upfront with the person as to why. If they have been taking advantage of your generosity and getting you to do their work, this is even more reason to say no, because continuing to say yes will eventually affect what you need to get done. If the person asking is a more junior staff member, it is important to look at why they are asking. Do they need more training, for example? Help them and make sure they understand this is a once-off.

You don't have to necessarily say no completely either. Instead, you can offer some information or guidance to help. You may connect them with other people in the business who might like the opportunity to work on an item or project and help guide them rather than you.

Saying no or yes is something we all deal with on a daily basis. I often get asked to participate in events and projects. My top tips that I practise are:

- I look at my main priorities first.

- I have to be passionate about what I am being asked to do and able to do it justice.

- There must be a realistic timeline.

- A quick no is a good no. Don't drag people on and think about it for weeks. Considering for 24 hours is long enough for most requests.

- Never say yes and then back out or miss a deadline because it will damage your brand.

Accepting a no

It's hard enough to say no, but how do you accept the no from someone else?

At a FEW conference, I was speaking to one of the speakers and we were discussing the importance of how you react when you receive a no. Both of us had had situations where people had wanted us to participate in things we were not available for. When we said no, they didn't take it well. The reaction to our no, which we felt had been delivered graciously, damaged the way we thought of the person taking the no.

If you are the recipient of a no, it is equally important to keep your composure, because you still have a stakeholder relationship to protect.

When I was building my executive search business years ago, potential clients responding with no was quite common. 'We are going to do it ourselves', they often said. If I had reacted by getting annoyed with them, I would have burnt very important bridges. Remember – sometimes a no is a cry for more information or they could just mean 'not right now'.

Taking the no in a gracious way will go a long way in keeping the relationship, maintaining your professionalism, and protecting your brand. Don't get mad and take your ball and bat home. It's definitely not a good idea to say things such as, 'Your loss, you will be sorry', 'We will take this to your competition', 'FINE', 'I can't believe you didn't go with us' (and then bag the competition), or 'You don't know what you are doing'. These types of comments will be seen as unprofessional and your reaction will be spread to others and will damage your brand.

Instead, accept it and leave the door open. Here are some tips for what to say when you are the recipient of a no response:

- 'Thank you for your consideration. I appreciate your time and please let me know if you change your mind. Could we keep the door open for the future and would you mind if I follow up in a few months to see if anything has changed?' This approach could be used, for example, in a situation where you have competed against someone else and lost the tender. You want to keep the connection in case they are not happy with their first decision. This would also assume you have answered all their questions, and this was the final no. This response could also be used for those times when you didn't get the job you were interviewing for.

■ 'I understand and appreciate your consideration. Thank you for your time and let me know if things change.' This simple acceptance of the no could be used when you have asked someone to participate in something – such as a project, additional task or even volunteer work.

Also keep in mind the no may be due to lack of adequate information. In the past, whenever I received a no for business, I would give the kind of response I've just outlined; however, I would also always ask the client if they could shed some light on why we lost the tender – for example, due to price, presentation or product. This helped us know what to improve on to give us a better idea in the future. Sometimes the reason for the no was as simple as they had a better relationship with someone else.

My view is that all relationships start out great. How many of your clients had a previous relationship before they started to work with you? If you burn your bridge with your first attempt to win business, it will be very hard to rebuild.

Take the no professionally and in the long term you might just win the yes.

CHAPTER EIGHT

No Sex With Your Mentor

Do you want to know why men are elevated to the top jobs in higher numbers than women? Do you think it is because women are discriminated against? Do you go into the interview process or your career feeling you are behind the eight ball? Are you convinced that sex has more to do with getting promoted than capabilities?

You will be surprised to know that discrimination may not be what is holding you back. Remember the old saying, 'It's not what you know, it's who you know'? The statement is still as relevant today – however, I have changed it slightly to 'It's who you know and how you access their help'.

The bottom line is you need people in your corner who are more senior in position than you are, and who can provide you with support and guidance throughout your career. You could try to progress by yourself, *but it will be a lot harder.*

Mentors: your personal board of directors

In my many years working in executive recruitment I noticed the T10Ps, and most men, have people in their corner guiding them through their career trajectory – including mentors, advocates, coaches, advisors. They are called by various names, but they all do one thing: they help you achieve your goals and make attaining success easier.

When I was recruiting, it was obvious that the guys had support in their corner. I could tell they had been briefed on what to do in every interview. They had knowledge about the person they were interviewing with – the kind of knowledge you can't get from a Google search. This valuable information would help them get over the line and give them the edge. Where did it come from?

This valuable information came from their mentors – people they had been collecting to guide them from the moment they took their first job. Every time they needed some advice, they would call them up to get their view and guidance on what move to make. They could basically act like a personal board of directors.

So, what type of information is so valuable that they call a mentor to find out? It's called *intel – information of political value.*

Wouldn't it be nice to go into an interview or a meeting with a potential client and know everything about that person? What if you knew the type of personality they had, their management style, how they viewed things and what not to do when you met them? Wouldn't that give you an edge? Yes, it does!

Call it fair or unfair, but this is what happens every day. Having people in your corner will give you not only an edge, but also a greater chance for success.

Remember the candidate who called the interviewer 'mate' in chapter 3? If only he had had a mentor to give him the intel on the interviewer. Such a mentor could have given him the heads up that the interviewer was not a person you get casual with and call 'mate'.

I founded FEW in 2011 because of everything I witnessed in running Financial Recruitment Group. I had been hearing about quotas for as long as I could remember and I was sick of it. The numbers were not dramatically changing for women in senior roles so something else needed to change.

As mentioned in chapter 2, I never felt that my clients were discriminating when deciding who to hire for the role. I believe the reason women were not getting more senior roles boiled down to a difference in support systems – mainly lack of mentors.

I found most men had mentors and most women didn't. It was so obvious why the men were progressing faster. Their mentors were helping them.

If a business has not one woman in a senior role, direct discrimination needs to be called out as the main cause. However, I personally know of hundreds of women who are in senior roles. If they did it, why can't others? If I did it, why can't others?

Most of us who have achieved have had mentors in our corner from an early age and through our careers.

Would I personally have achieved success if I didn't have mentors? Maybe, but it would have taken longer, and I probably would have made more mistakes along the way. So why make it harder for yourself?

REFLECTION

How many mentors do you have?

In the first year of FEW, we surveyed 100 of our senior members and asked them how many mentors they have had in their corner. Only two out of that group said they had a mentor.

Most respondents said that when they have a problem, they would ask a family member or casually ask a friend over drinks. Most of these women had already achieved a level of success, but still had a few more steps to go. The women at general manager level and above felt getting to the top had been hard and they wished they had had mentors to make the road easier and prevent some of the mistakes along the way.

In the survey, we also asked if the respondents kept in contact with early bosses – and, if not, why not? Responses often fell along gender lines. If the previous boss was a man, many women said something like, 'I didn't feel it was appropriate to keep in contact'; if the boss was a woman, they responded along the lines of, 'I don't want to bother her; she is too busy'.

We also surveyed 100 men from the FRG database, and they said they had between 7 and 12 mentors in their corner by the time they were in their first senior position. The men said they started to collect mentors early in their career. If they had a manager they liked who went to another area or company, they would keep in contact with them. Men did not care if their manager was male or female; if they liked them, they would keep in contact as one of their mentors.

If you needed career guidance today, who would you call outside your family or close friends? Are you making an effort to develop your own board of directors (that is, mentors)?

Why don't more women have mentors?

So why don't women collect mentors in the same way as the guys do early in their career?

Let's go back to early childhood and school days for someone to blame. Let's face it, these habits start early, and old habits are hard to break. At home or school, the boys likely had someone in their corner telling them what to do to prepare them for the big bad world of work.

Boys are encouraged to be brave, take chances, go outside the gate, play sport, be the breadwinner in the family, carry the load, fix things, not cry, get dirty, honour mateship and the 'bro code' along with numerous other pieces of advice.

Girls, on the other hand, were not given the same encouragement – and still aren't, even today. If no-one is in the household encouraging the girls that they can be whatever they want (as my grandmother and mother did), then encouragement will need to come from school or an external source. Mixed messages are all over the media for girls, but the boys' messages are pretty consistent due to historical behaviours.

So, yes, someone is to blame, as with most things we do in this world. But how do you want to deal with this – blame the past for the present, instead of just making the change now?

Blaming our upbringing for all our woes can only go on for so long, and when does it stop? Remember – our early mentors had mentors as well. The cycle needs to stop with early mentors, schools and social media working on taking the gender bias off the lens.

REFLECTION

Can you see the bias that existed in your own upbringing and childhood?

A friend of mine told me her daughter (in Year 12 at a well-known Australian private school), went on their offsite semester camp to a small regional town. On the last night, the boys were asked if they would like to invite their fathers for a campfire night, where they could carve horses together as a memento for the experience. The girls were asked to invite their mothers for a round circle event to talk about their feelings.

I couldn't believe what I was hearing and wondered why both groups couldn't do the same thing, or at least be given the choice. My friend said a small group of girls protested but nothing changed. These girls had strong role models at home who were teaching them to stand up for themselves when they saw an obvious sex divide. Those girls will be the ones who have the courage to stand up and speak out at work. They will probably also understand the importance of having good mentors.

It reminded me of when I was at school - girls had to take home economics and the boys took woodworking. It seems not so much has changed.

How could your school life and early career have been different if the sex divide had been removed?

By now, I hope you can see where I am going with this. Progressing in your career is more about identifying what you need to help you get there and how you do it, rather than the gender you were born with. A big part of that is seeking and taking help from mentors who will give you the guidance and support you need. People who help you achieve out of the goodness of their heart.

Often when I talk about this topic, someone says something along the lines of, 'Why do we need to change women?', so I will answer this now. We don't need to change women at all – women and men both need to understand the importance of mentors for their career. Your gender is not important; the behaviours you exhibit are.

Most men got the memo about mentors before women did. Women need to even the playing field and build up their mentor networks. This is not acting like a man or playing their game. This is about acting like the T10Ps. This is good business sense to get you from A to B, accessing help from those who have more experience. Those people who have already travelled that road before you and are now willing to give you directions.

What exactly does my mentor do?

The purpose of having advocates and mentors is to have someone as a fresh eye to give you guidance, support and advice based on experience from a career point of view. In addition, you're building your own personal board of directors you can access when needed.

What if you were given an IKEA bookshelf, flat-packed, and told to put it together, but when you opened the box there were no instructions? You could likely still figure it out and put it together, but it would take longer and might not look completely stable at the end (and you'll find those two extra screws). Mentors can help you put the shelf together faster and lessen the chance of any wobbles or you having a few screws loose.

To be clear: mentors are not people you call every week. They are people you can access confidentially who have your best interests at heart and are able to give you some guidance, support and experience when needed.

Some examples of when you would call your mentor include:

- for career guidance on what a next step could look like
- to get their views and/or support on a situation you are going through at work
- to run an idea past them for their view or to brainstorm
- to find out how to handle a performance review
- for advice and help with an interview

- for help when asking your boss for a salary increase

- when you've been approached for an opportunity and need to discuss it with someone confidentially

- for advice on how to handle an issue with a client when you don't want to ask your boss.

The proof is in the results

The first program that I developed at FEW was the Advocate Program. When a new member comes on board, they are paired with someone who is at least two levels higher than they are and who is outside of their current organisation. In turn, they are also paired to be an advocate for someone two levels more junior in position than they are. Our pairing process ensures they are paired with someone who will match what they need. That person is their advocate for at least 12 months and then they are re-paired with a new advocate.

Over the years we saw some amazing results through the Advocate Program. Here are some examples of how having a mentor helped some of our members.

> *My advocate gave me the gift of a new perspective. As she did not work within my organisation, it allowed us the freedom to have really honest conversations. At times our conversations were difficult as they involved a good deal of self-reflection, never easy but very valuable. Ultimately our conversations changed my mindset and my behaviour. I'm all the better for it.*

– Erica Hall, Morningstar

> *My advocate has helped me understand that we can be our own worst critics. She has helped me reflect on my career and experiences in the workplace and visualise the future. More importantly, she has given me the confidence after having my*

first child to keep developing myself, to value myself, reach out to my network and challenge myself. I feel like I have found a real friend in my advocate.

– Deline Jacovides, NGS Super

I've been so grateful for the time my advocate has given me, considering her busy role. It's been useful to have a third party – who is completely unbiased about your career and situation – listen and offer advice and guidance. She holds me to account so I know if I say I'm going to do something, I need to. I've learnt from her in terms of areas I need support with or advice – whether that be challenges I'm experiencing or purely a roadblock I'm struggling to overcome. She's made me think differently and implement things for my team that have worked well.

– Kate Bushell, QSuper

I couldn't have taken this new role without the support of some key mentors and advocates. It is easy to think you do not have all the skills you imagine you need to take on an opportunity when it is presented to you, and to then be overwhelmed when you do take the role on, but an advocate will help you work through these issues one on one as well as support you.

– Marisa Broome, Financial Planning Association (FPA)

REFLECTION

Are you comfortable helping others but uncomfortable asking for help?

Early in the building of FEW, we would contact, on a quarterly basis, the advocate and their sponsored person to see how they were going in the program. I thought that would be an appropriate time to follow up because I had given them the instructions on what to do and the timelines, so of course they had spent the last three months following my directions – wrong!

I contacted one of the most senior advocates we had (let's call her 'Jan'). Jan was a CEO of a very successful organisation and her sponsored person (let's call her 'Susi') should have felt privileged to have her as her advocate. Instead, Jan told me she hadn't heard from Susi since she received the introduction email three months ago. 'What?!' I said, because I couldn't understand why someone wouldn't take the opportunity to get guidance from this brilliant woman.

I decided, however, that before I contacted Susi, I would contact the person who Susi was an advocate to (let's call her 'Joyce'). When I called Joyce, she said, 'I love Susi! She is amazing and meets with me every month and follows up with calls as well'.

In case you are confused, this is what was happening. Susi was giving more time to Joyce than what was required as a commitment and not taking any time for herself. Sound familiar?! This is definitely a female behaviour that I have seen over and over: women giving more time to help others but not taking time for their own self-development. They were not born with this trait; they just haven't had the guidance from a mentor to tell them that they need to help and to be helped equally.

Men mentor others all the time; however, they know they need to get help as well – their mentors told them that! It's time for you to start thinking the same way.

Common mentoring questions

No doubt if you're new to the whole mentoring process (as many women are), you have a lot of questions. In this section, I answer some of the main ones I hear.

How many mentors do I need?

The number of mentors you need increases as you progress in your career. Here is a guide to the minimum number of mentors you should have according to your age:

- **If you're aged between 21 and 28 years:** You should have three mentors as a minimum.

- **If you're 29 to 42:** You need at least seven to nine mentors.

- **If you're over 43:** You need nine to twelve mentors, again as a minimum.

You might be surprised by how many mentors I recommend you have, but hear me out. Having a large group of mentors is important, so you can get multiple opinions and different perspectives depending on the issue at hand. Remember, you are trying to build your own personal 'board of directors' for your career, so you need to include people who can advise you in a wide range of situations.

In your board, look at having people with a variety of different backgrounds and experiences. That way, depending on the situation you need help with, you will have choices.

The end decision for any issue you have is yours, but wouldn't it be better if you had guidance from a range of different perspectives to draw from?

What makes a good mentor?

The first requirement for any mentor relationship is respect. You must respect the person you are asking to be your mentor. In addition, here are some criteria I suggest you review when deciding who to invite to be your mentor:

- Do they exhibit the qualities you aspire to?

- Do they have a background of success in the industry you are in? Or do they have expertise in an area you need help with?

- Are they stable in their career history, with good progression?

- Are they going to keep your information confidential?

- Do they have your best interests at heart?

People often ask me if it's better to choose a mentor from within your current organisation, or external to it. I always suggest working with an external mentor, because they will be able to talk to you more openly and will have fewer filters or worries about what they can or can't say. Unfortunately, internal mentors can't be as honest in their feedback as needed, for fear of being misunderstood or introducing issues that could affect their own position in the company. Remember the story of my early boss who said I was aggressive? He would probably be unlikely to tell me that today if we worked in the same organisation, and it was the feedback I needed to hear at the time.

Always remember that mentors give their time freely to help you. Most people are very happy to help and guide you, and feel flattered to be asked. The first step is to ask. The worst that could happen is they say no – and that's not the end of the world, because there will always be someone who will say yes.

I have had people ask me to be their mentors over the years and every time I see it as a compliment, not an annoyance. Again, think of how you would act if someone asked you. I can't mentor all of them and, when my schedule is full, I let them know. I also make sure they have a referral and encourage them to stay connected.

So where do I find these people called mentors?

Start your mentor search by making a list of all the people you know that you respect and who meet the criteria I've listed. Keep the list in a folder on your desktop for easy access, along with your stakeholder management plan, which I mentioned in chapter 4. Make note of who you contacted, the date and result.

Look at your past bosses who you admired and, if you haven't contacted them in a long time, reach out and touch base. LinkedIn is a good way to reconnect.

Then look at your LinkedIn network and see if you could formally approach anyone on it. Ask them if you could meet for a coffee and be upfront that you are connecting with people who you would like to consider as mentors in the future.

Mentoring is not a perfect science

Mentors do not have all the answers and their advice may not be right for you. They are basing their guidance on the path they travelled and what they learnt along the way. Take their background into consideration and weigh up the advice with everything else you have access to.

REFLECTION

How many people of the opposite sex do you have as mentors, or on your list as potential mentors?

In 2018, I launched FEW Good Men. As most senior positions are still held by men, the only way to break this cycle is for men to participate as mentors to the women who are coming up the ladder. Women in their thirties and forties are getting closer to the top of the ladder but, unlike their male counterparts, do not have the guidance, support and advice needed to help them take the next steps into the most senior level roles.

Most of the women we paired with the FEW Good Men stated that they had never had an advocate/mentor and the relationship has been life-changing for them. They feel that their advocate has really challenged them and helped them to look at things differently. All stated that they wish they'd had an advocate earlier in their career because it would have made their career life easier.

In developing both FEW and FEW Good Men, it has become very clear that mentorship comes from many areas of expertise. It is equally important for both women and men, and the gender of the mentor is irrelevant providing the mentor meets the mentor guidelines.

So don't forget to approach both sexes!

Making the most of mentorship

Every time you meet your mentor, record what you speak about and any next steps. Follow through on anything you've agreed to, and expect to be held to account. Also make sure to thank your mentors after you do meet by sending them a thank-you email for their time.

In a perfect world, winning a role or a promotion would be based just on the individual and their individual capabilities. I have given you the tips needed as an individual to do the best you can in your job; however, building your network and having mentors can really boost your individual performance – and is still up to you.

CHAPTER NINE

No Sex When Negotiating Your Worth

How much are you worth? Do you know? Are you underpaid? Are you afraid to ask for more?

Many people only have a vague idea of what they should be paid and largely accept whatever is offered. Most of these people are women. The fact that they are mainly women means women pay the price for their sex.

> **REFLECTION**
>
> Do you know the salary range for the position you're in now? What are you doing about it?
>
> Remember the story from chapter 1 of my mother finding out she was paid less than the men? The men she worked with told her about the unfairness – and that she should say something. Those men who gave her the 'heads up' were her mentors.

They had her back and saw how unfair it was – and gave her the encouragement to speak up.

Before this conversation, and being new to the workforce, my mother didn't know what was fair and what the market was paying. But she found out and did something about it.

Being naïve about what you are worth will open the door for you to be taken advantage of. Find out what the salary range is for your role, so you understand where you fit within it.

Women have been paying for their sex at work forever. The pay gap for women in 2020 in Australia is listed as 14 per cent. Why? We know that women are just as capable as men in all corporate roles, so why does inequality still exist? Is it direct discrimination? Is it because we don't speak up and negotiate?

It's all about negotiation

As a recruiter of senior executives, the reasons women were underpaid, that I observed, were less obvious than what we hear. Not once did any of my many clients offer the successful candidate less money because they were female. The salary range the company wants to hire at is determined upfront – before they know who they are going to hire.

What I did see was the men negotiating harder. They would ask for a salary that was over the range and, if the client really wanted them, the client would either try to get the range changed or offer an extra benefit that had a value – such as more holidays or flexible hours. Their mentors no doubt told them to go in hard – they weren't born knowing how to negotiate.

The female candidates would negotiate to a point, but not hard enough. They would accept roles at mid-range or towards the top of the range only if they had experienced a salary negotiation process before. They would be brave, but not confident.

Salary negotiations are when mentors can really add value. Because of their experience, they will have a better idea of how much you will be able to push your salary negotiations to. Doing your homework and asking for help could earn you thousands of dollars.

Negotiating for a pay increase in your current role

Say you have been in a role for 12 months or more and you think you should be paid more. 'I have done my job, so I deserve an increase', you say to yourself.

That may be true, but why? Did you go over and above your job requirements or are you just doing what is expected?

REFLECTION

Do you gather intel on your salary range before asking for an increase? Where do you get your intel from?

Several years ago we hired a junior staff member who, during her probation period, asked for an increase. Her manager said, 'You are still in your probation period and increases are not on the table for anyone until probation is over. Why do you feel you should have an increase?'

The staff member said, 'A friend of mine at an accounting firm said graduates should be on $10k more than what I am currently on'. Her manager replied, 'You are being paid a graduate rate plus two years' experience for a marketing role you haven't gained experience for. You can't compare this with what graduates in accounting get – we are actually paying you more than required'.

The junior staff member left and ended up going into accounting. The issue was that her intel was not correct for the role she was in. Getting advice from friends instead of mentors could result in making a wrong move. Leaving just for money or going to another role just for money is not a good move either.

Had she waited until her probation was over and put a logical case together to her manager with her achievements, she may have received an increase.

Consider why you deserve a pay rise and what you're actually after.

So many people think that simply because they have completed 12 months in a role, they are entitled to an increase. Increases come from achievements and going over and above what the role requires. The company is paying you to perform the position responsibilities on your position description and at a quality acceptable for the role.

When you meet with your manager for an increase, you need to show what you have done in your role that justifies an increase.

Negotiating at your performance appraisal

A good time to negotiate for a salary increase is at your performance appraisal.

Before the meeting, compile a list of your achievements from throughout the year. This is where keeping a folder on your computer called 'achievements' or 'wins' will come in handy. Every time you do something over and above your job requirement, record it and store it in this folder so you remember. When a client, customer or stakeholder emails you to thank you for something you have done, put it in that folder. All of this forms the 'why' – the evidence that justifies a salary increase.

You should also work out where you fit in the salary range for your role. If you don't know, ask your manager. Don't be shy or think it is an inappropriate question. This is your career, so why shouldn't you know?

Negotiating for a pay rise really is simple if you are prepared. Have everything that you have achieved written down. This answers the 'why?' Be upfront and say to your manager during the meeting that you would like to be considered for a salary increase. They will ask you, 'Why?' This is your opportunity to outline your reasons. You could say, for example, that in the last 12 months:

- 'I have exceeded my targets by 20 per cent.'

- 'I have mentored a junior staff member who is now fully trained.'

- 'In addition, I have brought on three new clients who have sent emails of appreciation.'

- 'I volunteered for a project that improved the administration system.'

Don't hesitate to ask for a salary increase. No-one will hold it against you and the worst thing that could happen is they say no.

If they say no, ask why. If they say not now, ask when. Most importantly, know how to communicate the reasons you should get the increase.

Negotiating a salary package for a new job

Say you have been offered a new job outside your current organisation and they ask what your salary expectations are.

By this stage in the process, you should know what the range is. If you don't, ask them about this before you answer.

If you find out the range is below what you are currently on, tell them! Say something like, 'That range is a lot lower than what I am on currently and I would be expecting an increase if I took the role'.

You need to decide what you are prepared to take. If the new role will give you more experience and the company is taking a chance on you – are you prepared to move sideways in salary or even take a drop? What is the benefit for you by doing this, and what value do you place on it?

Even if you don't have some of the role requirements, don't forget to highlight what you are bringing to the role. If the salary is lower than what you would like, but it will bring value to your background, those are considerations to think about and discuss with your mentors.

REFLECTION

Don't forget your package can include other benefits beyond the dollar amount.

Someone I mentor was going through a negotiation for a new role. She had been with her employer for many years. Negotiation was new to her and it made her feel uncomfortable to talk about money.

The recruiter she was dealing with gave her the offer and said it was best and final. She really wanted the role; however, the offer was exactly what she was currently being paid. She felt as if she had won the role but lost the salary package battle, and she questioned if she should take it.

The role was a great role and good for her career. However, my experience tells me that if people are unhappy with the salary package they accept, they will stew on it for months and that will have an impact on their transition into the company.

I told her negotiations were never over until the offer was signed. If the company gave a best and final offer and she was not happy with it, they might have other benefits they could offer that wouldn't add to the salary component. We discussed what she could ask for that would mean more to her than a $10k or $20k increase.

She went back to the recruiter and said, 'Could you let them know that I am really excited to accept this offer? However, the package is what I am on now. I understand that they are not in a position to go higher in dollars, so I have a proposal that I feel is a fair trade-off. An additional week's holiday at Christmas and a four-day week twice a month would make up for the lack of salary'.

She told the recruiter to reinforce why she would be good for the role and that she wasn't unhappy where she currently was. This meant she would want a more attractive package if she were to move. The company accepted the suggestions.

Is never hurts to ask and don't assume you will be knocked back. What could you negotiate that wouldn't cost the company in dollars but would have a value for you?

Here are some of the benefits you could negotiate with an employer when taking a new role if the salary is not suitable:

- additional annual leave

- a four-day week

- one day off per month

- hours 8.30 am to 4.00 pm (or something that works for you)

- a car parking spot

- working from home two days a week

- lowering the target for bonus payment

- a share option after probation

- a salary review in 12 months with an agreed percentage increase if targets are met.

Not all companies can increase the salary to make you happy, but they may be able to offer something else that will.

Accepting counteroffers

Imagine you have been offered an external position with another company. You go to your current boss to resign, but they don't want to lose you. In order to keep you from accepting another position, they offer you more money or additional benefits in an attempt to keep you happy, so you stay with them – you've accepted their *counteroffer*.

Accepting a counteroffer is a mistake from my point of view, and I always advise candidates to never accept one. If you have to resign to get what you deserve, perhaps you are in the wrong place.

Once a candidate was short-listed, I would tell them to have a good look at the role on offer and compare it with their current role. I would tell them that the new role had to be better than their current role – or why move?

I encouraged them to discreetly have a conversation with their current boss to get a feel about where their career was going within the organisation and what their future would look like. This way they could accurately compare the job on offer (which would in most cases be a step up) with the one they were currently in.

Every time I would emphasise, 'Don't accept this role and then be talked into a counteroffer by your current employer. Before you resign, compare the merit of both roles and decide which one will be better for your career, because counteroffers rarely work out'.

I would also explain that companies do not like to be put in the position of having to pay someone more money because they have threatened to resign. It makes them feel like they need to put a fire out and have been forced to act fast.

After the company has persuaded you to take the counteroffer and the dust settles, they will often start to resent what happened. They will remember when you said you had to go to the dentist – twice! They'll think about the day you dressed especially nicely and were out of the office for hours, and those (several) times you went into an office and closed the door. This all goes in the memory bank and when a downsizing comes up, who do they think of first?

In addition, where is the money for your counteroffer coming from? Is it from your bonus that they were going to pay you at Christmas – or the increase you should have gotten six months ago?

As a recruiter, I was not trying to scare the candidate out of accepting the counteroffer so they would take the role I was working on. I was trying to get them to see what I had seen over and over throughout the years. The internet is full of reasons not to accept a counteroffer, so do your homework, talk to your mentors and make your own decision. However, if it were me, I would make my decision about staying or going before it got to resignation stage.

REFLECTION

Along with considering how accepting a counteroffer might affect your current role over the long term, you also need to think about how the interviewers for the role you were going to accept will now think of you.

The best example of this (which is one of many) is when I was working on a general manager position in Sydney for a new client. I had presented my short-list and the client immediately pointed at one possibility and said, 'I wouldn't hire him in a million years!'

I was surprised and said, 'Why? He is a fantastic candidate! I have known him for years and he has a great reputation. He has been referenced-checked and all his achievements have been verified, so what is the issue?'

My client said, 'I offered him a role a few years ago, which he accepted, and then he accepted a counteroffer, so I will never hire him'.

Digging deeper, I found out that when he offered my candidate the role, my candidate was 26. At the time of the assignment, he was 42. I said to the client, 'Surely you aren't holding a grudge against a 26-year-old at the beginning of their career? That was 16 years ago'.

'Yes, I am', he said. 'It caused me a lot of problems and we had to start the process all over.'

Think about the damage you might be doing to your internal and external reputation – and the bridges you might be burning – before accepting a counteroffer.

People have long memories. How many of you still remember the bully at school who gave you a hard time? If you walked into an office and they were the person you were interviewing, how would your memory of having water thrown on you back in high school (for example) cloud your decision? Would ensuring this person didn't get the job be your revenge?

In the story in the previous Reflection, my client took his revenge on a candidate he felt had done the wrong thing by him in the past. The candidate had accepted an offer, and then knocked it back to take a counteroffer.

If you sign a contract and then back out, it is likely to haunt you years later.

I would always say to candidates, when they received a written offer, that they should make sure they were 110 per cent certain, because once they signed, the deal was done. If they backed out, it would damage their brand.

REFLECTION

Have you been tempted by a counteroffer in the past?

Over the years, I found female candidates were more likely to take counteroffers from their current employers. They thought it was flattering that their company wanted to keep them so much that they would fight for them. Most of the time money was not involved in the counteroffer, just empty promises of something that would happen.

Most of the men I dealt with had the attitude that if they'd accepted a new role and then their company tried to keep them, they were too late – they should have thought about that sooner. Counteroffers were very rare after a contract was signed and when they did accept one, they regretted it later.

Men not accepting counteroffers has a lot to do with access to more mentors who have travelled that road before and know the signs. They are able to give them the benefit of their experiences, so they don't make the same mistakes.

Who do you have in your corner that you can talk to about pay negotiations and counteroffers?

Signing the offer

Once you have signed an offer, your decision should be final. If you are going to accept a role verbally, this should be followed by:

I accept based on what we have discussed; however, this is subject to receiving a written letter and all the clauses being acceptable.

You need to read all the clauses in your letter and make sure you are happy with all of them. Your external mentors are great fresh eyes to run offers past and to look over anything you are not sure of. The more senior the role, the more complicated the offer will be. I would suggest seeking legal advice for any clause you do not understand.

Most people are so happy to get a role that they just skim over the clauses and sign the contract. I always ensured that I got the contract first from the client to look at, and then went over it with the candidate. I would recommend that they got advice for anything they didn't understand.

Some of the aspects that companies leave out in offer letters – because they are using a template – include:

- car parking details
- bonus structure
- agreed flexible hours or other flexible arrangements
- agreed review terms
- agreed targets and expense budgets
- relocation cost
- travel allowance.

Make sure that whatever payments and benefits you agreed to with the employer during the interview process are in writing for proof of promise. People forget the details of what they've promised or remember it differently, so make sure everything is in writing and everyone is on the same page.

Conclusion

My aim in writing this book was to demonstrate what the T10Ps do well, and provide lessons you can learn from these top performers to take into your own career. But the message I would really like to leave you with is this: *You are an individual.*

Don't let anyone discriminate against you in the work environment. Don't assume you will be held back from opportunities because of your sex. Focus on what you as an individual need to do to get from A to B, and learn the required skills.

If something happens that you are unsure of, ask for advice from your mentors. Have the courage to stand up for yourself and others, and to call out bad behaviour as it happens. Surround yourself with positive and experienced mentors to guide you at every step of the way.

Be thankful for critique and help from others, and learn from it. Help others to achieve their goals and be a role model. Build your brand as a leader and communicate with common courtesies. Don't levelise people: treat everyone equally.

The only identity you have is the one you make.

If I've inspired you to become a T10P, here are my final ten simple rules you should follow:

1. **Don't be a victim.** Don't blame the organisation, the systems, the culture, the economy, your boss or your

colleagues for your losses. Just get on with it. Fix what needs to be fixed and take accountability. Focus on what you do have, instead of what you don't have.

2. **Embrace confidence, not arrogance.** Don't feel the need to overstate your achievements. Don't levelise people, and don't be intimidated by people who are smarter than you are. Be respectful and always use the common courtesies.

3. **Be a leader.** Whether you're a people manager or not, you should always lead by example. Act ethically. Call out bad behaviour as it happens. Don't blame others for mistakes; take responsibility. See problems and find solutions. Make your staff work in an environment of responsibility and accountability.

4. **Build your brand.** Manage your stakeholders effectively. Understand the power of having a good reputation.

5. **Find your mentors.** T10Ps know that they can have it all – they just can't do it all. Build your team of advisors, mentors and coaches, and a personal board of directors. Don't be afraid to ask for help and show weakness.

6. **Deliver what you promise and communicate effectively.** Be true to your word. If you promise a deadline, deliver it. Return your calls and answer your emails.

7. **Delegate effectively.** Don't take the world on your shoulders. Give staff the opportunity to make mistakes and learn from them.

8. **Know your weaknesses.** Understand that you can't be good at everything, and bring in the right people.

9. **Balance work and life.** Don't work 24/7 – it's inefficient. To be efficient, you need to have a clear mind and healthy body. Make time for outside interests and have breaks from work.

10. **Do what you are passionate about.** To really be successful you need to love what you do, love where you work and see a future.

Thank you for reading *No Sex at Work*. I really appreciate the time you took to read my book. I hope you have been encouraged to continue in your career as an individual who can achieve anything you put your mind to. And if you initially thought *No Sex at Work* was about not having sex at work – well, don't do that either!

Author acknowledgements

I am sure I am not the only person who said they were glad to see the end of 2020. I had high hopes for 2020 and ended up experiencing extreme highs and extreme lows. The negativity that happened is the reason I buckled down and finally wrote *No Sex at Work*, which I had been planning to do for several years. I saw the best and worst of people this year and, in every circumstance, I feel it has made me a stronger person. I am grateful every day for the people who have been in my corner over the years, and especially the ones who rallied around me in 2020 giving me their support. They probably have no idea how valuable their support has been and how they helped turn a bad situation into a positive. It reinforced even more the importance of having a group of supporters in your corner.

Firstly, I would like to thank my husband and love of my life, Ron. Thank you for making me laugh every day and helping me put things into perspective with a fresh-eye approach.

Secondly, thanks to my group of go-to girls. My bff, Kellie Beggs, who has heard every up and down in my life since I was 16. Thank you for being in my corner and always listening and giving me great guidance. Krystyna Weston, who has also been in my corner since I started and continues to be not only a great friend but also a confidant who has helped me in many business situations. Anna Siassios, who for the past four years has been fantastic to work with and a great friend. You have always been supportive and always had my back. (I can't wait to see how your fabulous career continues to grow.) Also thanks to Ilaine, Tizzy, Barb, Geoff, Vanessa, Cris, Connie, Michelle, Amelia, Sue, Pene, Nigel, Luke, Dean, Mark, George and Mady, who have all been a great support in 2020 and prior years. Thank you for your words of support and wisdom.

This book would not have been written without my mother. She is the reason I have been able to achieve what I have. The picture I've included here was taken in December 2019, when she was 96 and visiting Australia from the US. Unfortunately, due to COVID, she was unable to travel again in 2020. How many people are still travelling at 96?! This should tell you something about her determination to live her best life and not let age or anything else stop her. What I have achieved is because of my mother, grandmother and father. Thank you for being such a wonderful role model and mentor. I cherish every moment we have had and appreciate everything you have done. xx

Also thanks to Lesley and the Major Street team, and to Charlotte Duff and Brooke Lyons for making writing the book a streamlined and fun process. And thank you Andrea Clarke for pushing me to call Lesley and get on with it! ☺

Contact the author

Thank you for reading my book, *No Sex at Work*. My hope is that you have taken away some valuable tips that will help you in your career journey. Sometimes information sinks in the first time and other times you need to re-fresh. Practice makes perfect, so don't think you have to get it right every time. I hope my book will be a guide for you at different times and stages of your career.

We know that Rome wasn't built in a day, and laying strong foundations takes effort with the help of a lot of people. Before publication, I gave this book to ten people who I consider Top 10 per centers (T10Ps) mentioned in the book. You will see their testimonials at the front of the book and I hope you share their views after reading. They inspired me to think what more could I do to start a movement of NSAW; a movement where we change attitudes across the board so people see other people as individuals. In addition, I wanted to provide a forum where people would learn how to be confident to take chances and believe in themselves.

This brought me to start the **NSAW book club**. The club will focus on delving into each chapter of this book via Zoom sessions and for members to ask questions in detail. This is a corporate initiative, structured to encourage organisations to include all their staff in the club and learn those important skills needed for everyone to progress in their career and become better humans and leaders. I will also bring in some of the T10Ps I have met over the years. If you are interested, please reach out to me via email for more details. Together we can ensure leadership does not become a gender.

I would also love for you to be part of my network on LinkedIn, Instagram and Facebook. Let me know if you have any questions and how your career is going. Networking is one of the most important parts of your journey and in today's digital environment it is so much easier to connect with people all over the world. You never know where your next opportunity will come from, or who will give you the right advice at the right time.

If you need a speaker at an event, please feel free to contact me. I love sharing my experiences with people.

I am here to help, so help me help you.

Regards
Judith

Email – judith@judithbeck.com.au
Website – www.judithbeck.com.au

Index

major st
PUBLISHING

We hope you enjoy reading this book. We'd love you to post a review on social media or your favourite bookseller site. Please include the hashtag #majorstreetpublishing.

Major Street Publishing specialises in business, leadership, personal finance and motivational non-fiction books. If you'd like to receive regular updates about new Major Street books, email info@majorstreet.com.au and ask to be added to our mailing list.

Visit majorstreet.com.au to find out more about our books and authors.

We'd love you to follow us on social media.

 linkedin.com/company/major-street-publishing

facebook.com/MajorStreetPublishing

instagram.com/majorstreetpublishing

@MajorStreetPub